ENDORSEMENTS

Ben Brown not only delivers the truth about praise and worship, but he lives to see others encounter the very presence of God. His book will challenge you to greater levels of understanding, so your church and ministry can move to a higher place. Interested in fostering genuine worship? Hungry for praise that frustrates the enemy and brings breakthrough? This book is for you!!!

—Glen Berteau
Author and Senior Pastor,
The House Modesto (thehousemodesto.com / glenberteau.com)

Ben Brown gives us a marvelous tool, in this book, to equip worshipers and local churches. As we lift the standard, may the name of Jesus be lifted high in all the earth!

—Bob Sorge
Author (bobsorge.com)

I am deeply stirred by my friend Pastor Ben Brown's new book, *People of His Presence*. This book is a clarion call back to the secret place where God has been waiting for His church to once again encounter a "deep calling unto deep" transformation. With very little hype, but great depth, Ben teaches us that worship is a lifestyle that starts in the womb of God's heart. This book is destined to be a feast for the hungry and a classic for the student! I highly recommend this book!

—Pat Schatzline
Author and Evangelist,
Remnant Ministries International (raisetheremnant.com)

Ben Brown just gave aspiring and current worship leaders a catapult forward with his new book, *People of His Presence*. Ben's articulation of worship practice and theology will provide the much-needed depth and understanding any leader needs, in order to be successful in today's church worship context. The foundational principles found in the pages of this book will serve worship teachers and students well for years to come!

—Dr. Mike Cuckler
Executive Director of Extended Education,
Southeastern University (seu.edu)

PEOPLE OF HIS PRESENCE

Foundational Studies in Praise and Worship

BENJAMIN BROWN

Copyright © 2017 Benjamin Brown.

Cover by Apollo Tull (Nice Tie Creative)

All rights reserved. No part of this book may be used or reproduced by any means, graphic, electronic, or mechanical, including photocopying, recording, taping or by any information storage retrieval system without the written permission of the author except in the case of brief quotations embodied in critical articles and reviews.

This book is a work of non-fiction. Unless otherwise noted, the author and the publisher make no explicit guarantees as to the accuracy of the information contained in this book and in some cases, names of people and places have been altered to protect their privacy.

Scripture taken from the HOLY BIBLE, NEW INTERNATIONAL VERSION®. Copyright © 1973, 1978, 1984 Biblica. Used by permission of Zondervan. All rights reserved.

Scripture taken from the HOLY BIBLE, KING JAMES VERSION®. Cambridge Edition, 1769. Public Domain.

Scripture taken from THE LIVING BIBLE®. Copyright © 1971 Tyndale House Foundation. Used by permission of Tyndale House Publishers, Inc. All rights reserved.

Please note: Scriptures are taken from the New International Version unless otherwise indicated.

WestBow Press books may be ordered through booksellers or by contacting:

WestBow Press
A Division of Thomas Nelson & Zondervan
1663 Liberty Drive
Bloomington, IN 47403
www.westbowpress.com
1 (866) 928-1240

Because of the dynamic nature of the Internet, any web addresses or links contained in this book may have changed since publication and may no longer be valid. The views expressed in this work are solely those of the author and do not necessarily reflect the views of the publisher, and the publisher hereby disclaims any responsibility for them.

Any people depicted in stock imagery provided by Thinkstock are models, and such images are being used for illustrative purposes only.
Certain stock imagery © Thinkstock.

ISBN: 978-1-5127-7757-4 (sc)
ISBN: 978-1-5127-7758-1 (hc)
ISBN: 978-1-5127-7756-7 (e)

Library of Congress Control Number: 2017903589

Print information available on the last page.

WestBow Press rev. date: 6/23/2017

Preface

It was a typical Sunday evening about twenty years ago. Those were the services that could go a little longer because no one was under any time constraint, and no one wanted to be anywhere else. We had gathered to experience God, and electricity was in the air as the congregation began lifting up songs of praise and worship.

I was amazed at how He would make Himself known among that congregation in central Illinois. The people of Pawnee Assembly would praise passionately, worship intimately, and God would show up. We were about forty-five minutes into this particular worship time, and a holy hush had come over the entire room. No one dared say a word, as we all waited on the Lord. Some were standing, and others were lying prostrate on the floor, but *all* were captured by His presence.

This is where I cut my worship-leading teeth. It's where I learned what praise and worship is all about. The church had undergone many changes, including a transition from song service to praise and worship experience. Our pastor, Patrick Rusch, had developed a sermon series, "People of His Presence," which developed into a twelve-week discipleship class that revolutionized our church and caused otherwise ordinary saints to become extravagant worshipers.

When I first laid eyes on that original "People of His Presence" teaching, I knew my pastor had stumbled onto something that could make a significant impact, not only in our church, but in the church at large. During the last several years, we have seen a worship renewal in the greater evangelical church, yet I am amazed at the lack of in-depth teaching about praise and worship, and its importance to the life of any congregation. Seeing the need to get these truths in as many hands as possible, I began editing and expanding the "People of His Presence" teaching with my pastor's blessing. I am forever indebted to him for his groundbreaking study and am excited to unveil a comprehensive yet straightforward approach to praise and worship for the local church.

The material you are about to read has transformed the lives of pastors, worship teams, and average men and women in churches across America. I have personally ministered to congregations all over the United States, and every time this teaching has been presented, breakthrough has come because people have discovered their purpose as worshipers. They've learned to be people of His presence!

Acknowledgments

Patrick Rusch, thank you for breaking ground with your "People of His Presence" sermon series and discipleship program. I am forever indebted to you for laying an important foundation that has led to the writing of this book.

Jill Brown, thank you for your unending love and support as we've worked tirelessly on this project. I could not have done this without you.

Contents

Chapter 1
GETTING STARTED

Do you want to develop a deeper passion for God?

Are you longing for more of His presence in the church?

Have you ever wondered *why* we do *what* we do during the first twenty to thirty minutes of contemporary worship services?

If you answered yes to any or all of the questions above, this teaching is for you! The fact of the matter is, God *wants* to give you a deeper passion for the things on His heart. He *wants* to increase your awareness of His living presence, and He *wants* you to discover the truth about praise and worship because that discovery is a key to fulfilling your purpose and unlocking your potential, as a child of the King of kings.

So what exactly is "praise and worship"? Most evangelical believers will recognize the term, which came into use during the Charismatic Renewal of the '60s and '70s, and gained widespread popularity during the Worship Movement of the late '90s and beyond. However, though many recognize the term, few understand all that it implies. Keep reading, because you are about to discover that praise and worship is much more than singing songs during a Sunday morning worship service. True and wholehearted praise and worship will change you from the inside out!

So let's define praise and worship. In order to understand what it *is*, we first need to understand what it *isn't*.

Emotionalism

In some congregations, we encounter emotionally driven praise and worship. Responses are based entirely on feelings, and the atmosphere seems to be charged with hype. This type of praise and worship easily lends itself to extremes.

Traditionalism or Intellectualism

In other congregations, praise and worship errs on the side of heartless tradition or mental ascent. Traditions in and of themselves are not bad, but when those traditions become meaningless, true devotion is sabotaged. Similarly, we've been given the ability to think with our minds, and that is not a bad thing. Still, we must be careful that praise and worship doesn't degenerate into a mental exercise.

Trivializing Praise and Worship

Another common mistake is to view praise and worship as warm-up music—what we do to get people to realize the church service is starting, so they'll come in and find a seat. Or it's musical entertainment—something the people observe but don't actively participate in. Finally, it can become a preliminary to the "real thing"—the preaching of the Word. Not only is this unscriptural, but it's like going to someone's house for dinner and viewing your relationship with that person as secondary and preliminary to getting what you really want—dinner! True praise and worship should actually be seen on an equal plane with the preaching of the Word or reading of the Word for two reasons:

> Ephesians 2:19–22: "Consequently, you are no longer foreigners and aliens, but fellow citizens with God's people and members of God's household, built on the foundation of the apostles and prophets, with Christ Jesus himself as the chief cornerstone. In him the whole building is joined together and rises to become a holy temple in the Lord. And in him you too are being built together to become a dwelling in which God lives by his Spirit."
>
> Romans 15:5–6: "May the God who gives endurance and encouragement give you a spirit of unity among yourselves as you follow Christ Jesus, so that with one heart and mouth you may glorify the God and Father of our Lord Jesus Christ."
>
> 1 Peter 2:9: "But you are a chosen people, a royal priesthood, a holy nation, a people belonging to God, that you may declare the praises of him who called you out of darkness into his wonderful light."

1. Biblical praise and worship is a primary means by which we minister to God as New Testament priests. We were created to glorify Him, not just listen to sermons. (See Ephesians 2:19–22, Romans 15:5–6, and 1 Peter 2:9.)

2. Biblical praise and worship should *be* or *be based on* the Word of God!

Biblical Praise and Worship

We often hear that worship is a lifestyle—and it *is*. Let me say, I am grateful for church leaders and theologians who have brought needed balance in this area, causing us to realize that worship is more than what we do in church services on Sunday morning. Nevertheless, I think we can swing the pendulum too far the other direction, and worship can be *anything but* the musical acts of devotion that are commonly associated with praise and worship. For instance, if I am not a singer, can't I be excused from participation in praise and worship, and instead, can't I worship God some other way—through something I'm good at? This is a common argument, but it is certainly not the biblical paradigm, as we will see.

Please don't misinterpret what I'm saying. If you are a skilled craftsman, you can worship God each time you build something at your workbench. But this doesn't excuse you from engaging in a very important form of corporate devotion—musical praise and worship.

True, worship was never restricted to musical forms or rituals in Old and New Testaments, but scripture repeatedly linked God-honoring music to worship, and powerful things happened when believers lifted up their voices together in song. Reality is, music touches the soul in ways spoken word cannot, and music is one of the most effective means of bringing a room together. God knew this from the beginning, and that's why musical praise and worship has been such an important part of our devotion throughout the ages.

Based on descriptions of what praise and worship *isn't*, and based on how we've demonstrated the importance of musical acts of devotion, we can provide a simplified working definition as follows, which will be the foundation for the rest of this study:

Praise and worship is a living interaction between God and His worshipers, as experienced through musical arts.

Don't get me wrong. Music does not equal worship, but music is a strategic tool we use to foster a two-way dialogue, to enhance the rhythm of revelation and response, as God is revealing Himself, and people are responding to His presence.

Let me close this chapter with one final thought. I've often heard it said that praise and worship is *caught* more than it's *taught*. While there's some truth to this, I don't think the statement is entirely accurate. One's ability to praise and worship the Lord correctly, I believe, is directly linked to (1) exposure and (2) understanding. Yes, we must set a visible example before people and urge them to plunge into the experience. But if people aren't taught what we are trying to accomplish during times of praise and worship—if they aren't taught what their God-given role is during those times—then we shouldn't expect them to do it properly.

So let's gain the right understanding alongside the right experiences. As we start this journey, let me encourage you to set aside your preconceived notions and embrace what God's Word says about praise and worship. In doing so, your life will be forever impacted, and you will be that son or daughter He's called you to be—and together, we will truly become *people of His presence.*

Devotional Exercise

Throughout this next week, meditate on the truths of this opening lesson. Ask the Lord to prepare your heart for receptivity of His Word, and also to open your eyes of understanding as truth is revealed over the next several chapters.

Study Guide Questions—Chapter 1

1. Describe the difference between emotionalism and biblically motivated praise and worship that utilizes our emotions.

2. What are some ways a person might revive songs that have lost their meaning or become lifeless?
3. In your own words, describe how praise and worship should be a living interaction between God and His worshiper(s).

Chapter 2

THE PROXIMITY OF OUR WORSHIP

Proximity. That's a big word! What does it mean?

In this study, it has to do with where we are at any given point in our worship journey, in relation to God. The pathways into the presence of God need to be well traveled so we can become familiar with our surroundings and learn to function and flow in an atmosphere of praise and worship.

In the same way a well-studied and well-traveled explorer knows the silhouette of each mountain and the bend of each river—just as he's familiar with each fallen tree and every landmark along the path—the people of God ought to know the pathways of His presence so they can function properly as His worshipers.

In this chapter, we'll begin to discover the proximity of our worship. It will be helpful, though, to first describe some differences between *praise* and *worship*. The two obviously function together, but their roles differ somewhat.

Please understand, what I'm about to say isn't entirely black and white. Definitions generally apply, but they aren't absolutely clear-cut.

Recognizing occasional exceptions, let's define the two terms as follows.

The Lord enjoys our *praise*, but He doesn't need it; (all creation continually praises Him whether we choose to or not). Furthermore, praise can be somewhat distant, where individuals talk about God but not directly to Him. It is often horizontal in nature, or person-to-person. Finally, true praise is always seen or heard.

On the other hand, the Lord seeks *worshipers*; He needs them, not because He lacks anything, but because He longs for a relationship with people. And worship is intimate, where individuals address God directly. It is typically vertical in nature, or person-to-God. Finally, true worship is most importantly a function of the heart, which means it may or may not be seen or heard. What's important is that the worshiper is responding to the Lord in obedience.[1]

I don't want you to get the impression that I place little value on praise because it is less intimate. Praise has a very important function, actually preparing people to come into a more intimate dialogue with God. Praise brings a healthy balance to corporate worship times, too, so they are not just "God and me" experiences, but people are actively drawn into right relationship with those around them. The New Testament calls us to strengthen one another as we gather, and healthy praise will cause people to build each other up—to encourage each other to praise God for who He is and what He does—versus simply having individual worship experiences where there is no investment in each other's lives.

This being said, I must make the following point. While virtually anyone can praise (all creation, in fact, praises the Creator), only those who know the Lord can truly worship Him. The praise and worship experience is primarily for the believer because the whole point is to foster a living interaction, a dialogue, a relationship between God and the worshiper.

Against this backdrop, let's explore the Old Testament pattern of the tabernacle to further understand proximity.

1. Praise and worship was at the heart of Exodus.

In the Old Testament, Moses was God's agent for revealing the pathway into God's presence (in terms mankind could understand).

---

[1] Adapted from *Exploring Worship: A Practical Guide to Praise & Worship*, by Bob Sorge (Lee's Summit, MO: Oasis House, 2000), 67–72.

As the Lord spoke to Moses on Mount Sinai, He not only gave him the Ten Commandments, but also a very detailed description of the tabernacle, or dwelling place that was to be built. This is where the Lord would dwell in a very real and physical way among His people. (Notice that the tabernacle was for the entire nation, not just for individuals. This was a significant step forward in the worship practices of Israel, because up until this point, worship had predominantly consisted of individual sacrifice.)

> Exodus 25:40: "See that you make them according to the pattern shown you on the mountain."

The account of Moses's interaction with God on the mountain is contained in Exodus chapters 19 through 31. The specific instructions concerning the tabernacle and its furniture are found in Exodus 25 to 27. In these instructions, God is very articulate and careful to make sure Moses understands that everything is to be done exactly right, according to the pattern shown to Him. (Refer to Exodus 25:40.)

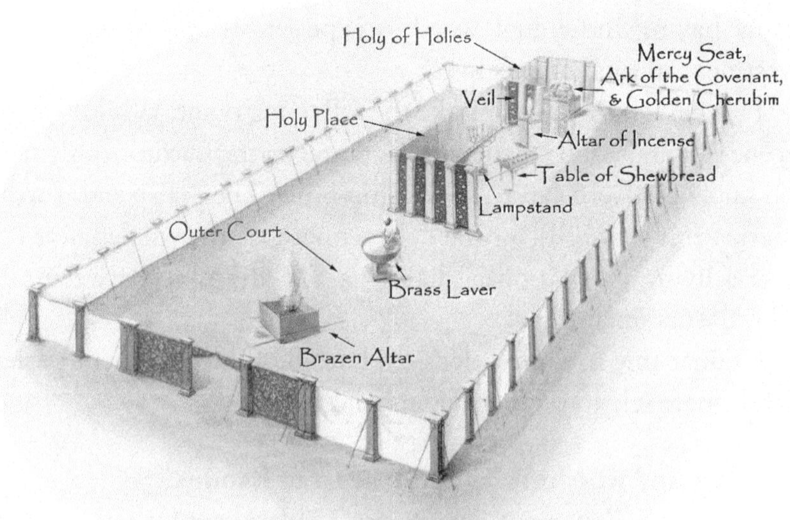

Tabernacle of Moses

2

---

[2] John Robert Lucas Ministries, copyright 2011. Accessed at www.templebuildersministry.com.

The physical structure depicted on the previous page was at the center of the tribal arrangement, which signifies God's desire to be at the center of His people's lives. Notice the design: three separate rooms, each with its own distinct articles of furniture.

Once a year, on the Day of Atonement, the high priest, having gone through all his priestly duties, would take the blood of the sacrifice, representing the sins of the people, through the veil, where he would enter (along with incense) into the holy of holies to meet with God.

The blood of the sacrifice would be sprinkled on the mercy seat, signifying that a sacrificial death had taken place for the people, and their sins for the entire year had been atoned (paid for).

Only the high priest could pass through the veil and into the holy of holies, and only once a year, on the Day of Atonement—and even then, not without sacrificial blood. He had to completely satisfy all the requirements. Otherwise, he would be struck down in the presence of God.

(The high priest had bells attached to the bottom of his robe and a rope attached to his ankle. If at any time the bells became silent, it could be assumed that something had happened, and the priest had died. If anyone would enter the holy of holies to retrieve the body, he too would die. So the dead body would be pulled from the tent with the rope.)

2. The tabernacle was given as a replica or "shadow" of the reality in heaven.

In Hebrews, the writer explains that the tabernacle in the wilderness was a physical replica of a heavenly reality—the dwelling place of God, or His throne room. This is why the details were important. God wanted to give an accurate picture so His people would recognize the reality yet to be revealed in the New Testament through Christ…

"They [Old Testament priests] serve at a sanctuary that is a copy and shadow of what is in heaven. This is why Moses was warned when he was about to build the tabernacle: 'See to it that you make everything according to the pattern shown you on the mountain'" (Hebrews 8:5).

Interestingly, the tent and articles of furniture were arranged in the shape of a cross, foreshadowing all that Christ came to accomplish on mankind's behalf. Also, many elements of the tabernacle corresponded with various ministries of Christ, as the following table illustrates:[3]

TABERNACLE ELEMENT	MINISTRY OF CHRIST
The tablets of stone in the Ark	Christ as the Living Word, Who came to fulfill the law and establish a new covenant
The golden pot of manna in the Ark	Christ as the Bread of Life, Who meets every one of our needs
Aaron's budding rod in the Ark	Christ's defeat of death and resurrection from the dead on the third day
The Mercy Seat	Christ as the Lamb of God, Who shed His blood to take away the penalty for our sins
The table	Christ's humanity, One Who sat among His disciples and fellowshipped with them
The lampstand	Christ's untainted and invaluable deity, as pure and priceless gold
Oil for the lamps of the lampstand	Christ's continued ministry in a darkened world, through the power of the Holy Spirit
The veil	Christ's body torn so mankind could pass through the veil that separates unholy people from a holy God
The purple, scarlet, and blue colors of the curtains	Christ's attributes of royalty, shed blood, and heavenly kingdom

In addition, the Old Testament high priest was a picture (although imperfect) of Christ, our true High Priest, who *Himself* became our sacrifice for sin upon the cross…

> The law is only a shadow of the good things that are coming—not the realities themselves. For this reason it can never, by the same sacrifices repeated endlessly year after year, make perfect those who draw near to worship. If it could, would they not have stopped being offered? For the worshipers would have been cleansed once for all, and would no longer have felt guilty for their sins. But those sacrifices are an annual reminder of sins, because it is impossible for the blood

[3] Vernon M. Whaley, *Called to Worship: The Biblical Foundations of Our Response to God's Call* (Nashville, TN: Thomas Nelson, 2009), 232–33.

> of bulls and goats to take away sins. Therefore, when Christ came into the world, he said: "Sacrifice and offering you did not desire, but a body you prepared for me; with burnt offerings and sin offerings you were not pleased." Then I said, "Here I am—it is written about me in the scroll—I have come to do your will, O God." First he said, "Sacrifices and offerings, burnt offerings and sin offerings you did not desire, nor were you pleased with them" (although the law required them to be made). Then he said, "Here I am, I have come to do your will." He sets aside the first to establish the second. And by that will, we have been made holy through the sacrifice of the body of Jesus Christ once for all (Hebrews 10:1-10).

The next two verses further clarify this once for all sacrifice…

"Day after day every [Old Testament] priest stands and performs his religious duties; again and again he offers the same sacrifices, which can never take away sins. But when this priest [Jesus Christ] had offered for all time one sacrifice for sins, he sat down at the right hand of God" (Hebrews 10:11–12).

The fact that Jesus Christ became our sacrifice (usually an innocent, spotless animal whose lifeblood was shed in place of the guilty individual) explains why He is referred to as the "Lamb of God" in scripture. Notice also the words of John and the worshipers around the throne in heaven as described in Revelation chapter 5…

"Then I saw a Lamb, looking as if it had been slain, standing in the center of the throne, encircled by the four living creatures and the elders. In a loud voice they [worshipers] sang: 'Worthy is the Lamb, who was slain, to receive power and wealth and wisdom and strength and honor and glory and praise!' Then I heard every creature in heaven and on earth and under the earth and on the sea, and all that is in them, singing: 'To him who sits on the throne and to the Lamb be praise and honor and glory and power, for ever and ever!'" (Revelation 5:6, 12–13).

3. The significance of Jesus's death was demonstrated.

The significance of Jesus's death as our sacrificial Lamb was powerfully demonstrated while He was on the cross and prepared to breathe His last, the cross itself being a fulfillment of the altar of sacrifice in the tabernacle of Moses.

> John 19:30: "When He had received the drink, Jesus said, 'It is finished.' With that, he bowed his head and gave up his spirit."
>
> Matthew 27:51: "At that moment the curtain of the temple was torn in two from top to bottom. The earth shook and the rocks split."
>
> Hebrews 4:15–16: "For we do not have a high priest who is unable to sympathize with our weaknesses, but we have one who has been tempted in every way, just as we are—yet was without sin. Let us then approach the throne of grace with confidence, so that we may receive mercy and find grace to help us in our time of need."

He cried out, "It is finished" (John 19:30), which is a Greek expression used regularly in those days at the marketplace.

When a purchase was made at the marketplace, people would say this word—*tetelestai*—which simply meant: The transaction is finished—completed. The debt is paid in full! As Jesus was saying, "It is finished," He was declaring that the debt of our sin was being paid in full, and His substitutionary work as a sacrifice had been completed.

At this very moment, the veil (or curtain in the Jewish temple) still separating the holy place from the holy of holies was torn from top to bottom (Matthew 27:51).

This was extremely significant because, through the tearing of the veil, God was saying to mankind: "I accept the blood of this innocent, spotless, sacrificial Lamb as payment in full for your sin."

Now, *all* believers at *any* time have access to the very throne-room of God (Hebrews 4:15–16).

Remember, it is the Holy Spirit who now takes up residency in your heart…

"Because you are sons, God sent the Spirit of His Son into our hearts, the Spirit who calls out, 'Abba, Father'" (Galatians 4:6).

Jesus Christ has ascended into heaven, where He is seated upon the throne in His glorified, physical body, at the Father's right hand…

"That power is like the working of his mighty strength, which he exerted in Christ when he raised him from the dead and seated him at his right hand in the heavenly realms, far above all rule and authority, power and dominion, and every title that can be given, not only in the present age but also in the one to come" (Ephesians 1:19–21).

And we have been given free access to this place where Jesus and the Father reside...

"And God raised us up with Christ and seated us with him in the heavenly realms in Christ Jesus" (Ephesians 2:6).

What is the throne room like?

Perhaps the best description of the throne room in heaven, and what goes on there, is found in the narrative of the events described in Revelation chapters 4 and 5. Take a moment right now and read John's vision of the throne room in Revelation chapter 4...

> After this I looked, and there before me was a door standing open in heaven. And the voice I had first heard speaking to me like a trumpet said, "Come up here, and I will show you what must take place after this." At once I was in the Spirit, and there before me was a throne in heaven with someone sitting on it. And the one who sat there had the appearance of jasper and carnelian. A rainbow, resembling an emerald, encircled the throne. Surrounding the throne were twenty-four other thrones, and seated on them were twenty-four elders. They were dressed in white and had crowns of gold on their heads. From the throne came flashes of lightning, rumblings and peals of thunder. Before the throne, seven lamps were blazing. These are the seven spirits of God. Also before the throne there was what looked like a sea of glass, clear as crystal. In the center, around the throne, were four living creatures, and they were covered with eyes, in front and in back. The first living creature was like a lion, the second was like an ox, the third had a face like a man, the fourth was like a flying eagle. Each

> of the four living creatures had six wings and was covered with eyes all around, even under his wings. Day and night they never stop saying: "Holy, holy, holy is the Lord God Almighty, who was, and is, and is to come." Whenever the living creatures give glory, honor and thanks to him who sits on the throne and who lives forever and ever, the twenty-four elders fall down before him who sits on the throne, and worship him who lives forever and ever. They lay their crowns before the throne and say: "You are worthy, our Lord and God, to receive glory and honor and power, for you created all things, and by your will they were created and have their being" (Revelation 4:1–11).

Here's the significance of this. The tabernacle in the wilderness (Moses's tabernacle) was established among the people of God to give us a picture, or replica, of the reality in heaven. Revelation chapter 4 describes this reality—the true throne room that exists in the heavenly realms right now! The pathway of the Old Testament priests moving from the outer court through the veil and into the immediate and intimate presence of God typifies the reality of our progression as we draw close to God in praise and worship. God has removed the veil because of the blood of Jesus, who became our perpetual sacrifice for sin (perpetual because of the continuing effects of His work of redemption, not in the sense that He has been sacrificed over and over).

Is it really possible?

Can we as believers really sense our entry into this place? The answer is yes! Through praise and worship, we've been given the privilege of entering in any time we choose.

Still unconvinced? Well, Dr. Jack Hayford (to whom we are incredibly indebted for his ground-breaking work in praise and worship study) tells of an eye-opening experience he had early in his ministry at the Church on the Way in Van Nuys, California.

While the church was still small, he and his staff were praying in the sanctuary one Saturday evening. The Holy Spirit spoke to Pastor Jack, to have the staff separate into each of the four corners of the sanctuary and resume worship. After some hesitation and reluctance, Pastor Jack submitted to the Spirit's direction. As worship continued, each staff member in each corner of the sanctuary became increasingly aware of an angelic presence.

Two weeks later, Pastor Jack felt compelled to have his staff again position themselves at the four corners, and this time, the youth pastor received a vision of four angelic beings, one stationed at each corner.

Then, several days later, during an early-morning prayer meeting, the Lord again reminded Pastor Jack of the four angelic beings. Curious to know the meaning of all three experiences and the significance of these angelic beings, Pastor Jack was drawn to the passage we read above (Revelation 4), as well as Psalm 22:3…

"But thou art holy, O thou that inhabitest the praises of Israel." (KJV)

The Hebrew word for "inhabitest" is *ya-shab*, which means "to sit down; to dwell, to remain; to marry; to (make to) abide, establish, inhabit, or seat."[4]

The New International Version translates Psalm 22:3 this way…

"You are enthroned as the Holy One."

The point that the Lord impressed upon Pastor Jack's heart is this: the Holy One dwells in the midst of (or upon) the praises of His people as He is seated on His throne among them.[5]

Interestingly, notice the description of the reality of the heavenly throne room given to us by John in Revelation 4…

"At once I was in the Spirit, and there before me was a throne in heaven with someone sitting on it" (Revelation 4:2).

---

[4] *Yashab* (Strong's Hb3427) as defined in *A Concise Dictionary of the Words in the Hebrew Bible with Their Renderings in the Authorized English Version* (Nashville, TN: Abingdon Press, 1973), 52.

[5] Adapted from *Glory on Your House*, by Jack W. Hayford (Grand Rapids, MI: Chosen Books, 1991), 82–91.

Remember the Holy Spirit's lesson to Pastor Jack? As each staff member worshiped the Lord in the four corners of the sanctuary, each became aware of an angelic presence. Now recall verse 6 of John's throne room vision in Revelation 4…

"Also before the throne there was what looked like a sea of glass, clear as crystal. In the center, around the throne, were four living creatures, and they were covered with eyes, in front and in back."

Could it be that the angelic presence felt by each staff member was none other than that of the heavenly host in the heavenly throne room? Could it be that we as New Testament believers, having been granted access by the blood of Jesus Christ into the real holy of holies—we who engage in priestly duties, offering praise and worship to the Lord—are actually translated *in our awareness* to a heavenly dimension, where the glorified Christ is seated in our midst and God is enthroned as the angelic creatures continually offer praise and worship?

Confirmation in Isaiah

This was *exactly* the prophet Isaiah's experience…

"In the year that King Uzziah died, I saw the Lord seated on a throne, high and exalted, and the train of his robe filled the temple. Above him were seraphs, each with six wings: With two wings they covered their faces, with two they covered their feet, and with two they were flying" (Isaiah 6:1–2).

Notice the similarities in what the angelic beings were saying…

"And they were calling to one another: 'Holy, holy, holy is the Lord Almighty; the whole earth is full of his glory'" (Isaiah 6:3).

"Day and night they [the four living creatures] never stop saying: 'Holy, holy, holy is the Lord God Almighty, who was, and is, and is to come'" (Revelation 4:8).

Scripture tells us that God is omnipresent; He is everywhere. Yet, as we have learned, He does dwell in the midst of His people. And at times, he manifests Himself in greater glory.

Separated by Awareness, Not Distance?

Could it be that we are separated from those heavenly realms, the place of God's manifest presence, more because of *awareness* (choice and desire not to enter) than mere *distance*?!

A. W. Tozer, pastor, scholar, and Christian statesman, writes:

"The Presence and the manifestation of the Presence are not the same. God is here when we are wholly unaware of it. He is manifest only when ... we are aware of His Presence. On our part, there must be surrender to the Spirit of God, for His work is to show us the Father and the Son. If we cooperate with Him in loving obedience, God will manifest Himself to us, and that manifestation will be the difference between a nominal Christian life and a life radiant with the light of His face."[6]

Tozer goes on to say that our pursuit of God must include prayers for increasing degrees of awareness, and our spiritual receptivity must be cultivated.

A Matter of Progression and Attitude

This being said concerning the proximity of our worship—that is, the nearness of God's manifest presence to His worshipers—chapter 2 concludes with these thoughts:

As we approach God in praise and worship, there is a distinct pathway that we follow (as was the case in the earthly shadow—the tabernacle of Moses). Don't misunderstand. What I'm about to describe is not a rigid construct, with hard-line barriers between one section of the path and another. Still, the following progression serves as a protocol for our entry into that place where we are made aware of His manifest presence.

---

[6] A. W. Tozer, *The Pursuit of God* (Harrisburg, PA: Christian Publications, 1948), 64.

Psalm 100:4: "Enter his gates with thanksgiving and his courts with praise; give thanks to him and praise his name."

As we come in from the outside (i.e., the world and all of its distractions), we pass through His "gates" with thanksgiving and head into His "courts" with praise. (See Psalm 100:4.)

- First, we enter the outer court. This was/is a place of less intimacy with God. It's where we are more conscious of one another. Also, this is usually where we praise the Lord, singing to one another about God or one of His attributes. Meanwhile, the Holy Spirit begins to whittle away at what's wrong on the inside of us, to prepare us to go deeper.
- Second, we progress into the holy place. Here, our focus on God becomes deeper and more intense. This is where the transition from praise to worship usually takes place, and where we begin to become more aware of His habitation.
- Third, we pass through the veil that has been opened by the blood of Jesus and come into the holy of holies, the very throne room of Almighty God. This is the place of greater intimacy, where we're totally captivated with the Lord. It is here that we truly worship Him, no longer simply singing about Him, but singing to Him directly.

Please note that the progression I've just described is not a magic formula for translating us into a "holy of holies encounter" with God. Where we are at a given point in the journey is largely dependent upon whether we have entered in, either individually or corporately. (In other words, we can sing intimate songs at a given point and still be "far off" because we have not willfully and intentionally taken steps into a deeper place with God.)

Still, while the progression is not a magic formula, it is definitely one of the clearest pictures God gave us of the proper way to approach His presence.

The next chapter focuses on our responsibility to enter in, and the things that can stand in the way. As chapter 2 closes, I encourage you to think about this: *the attitude with which you come will determine the depth in which you go.*

Summation

1. "Praise" and "worship" are essentially two sides of the same coin. They function together in church services, but serve different roles.
2. The Old Testament tabernacle in the wilderness, as well as various priestly duties, all serve as shadows, or replicas of realities in the heavenly realm.
3. Through Jesus's sacrificial death, the veil separating God's people from His immediate presence was opened.
4. As we praise and worship, Jesus Christ is enthroned in our midst, upon our praise.
5. We enter into the heavenly throne room, the true holy of holies, where we encounter God's manifest presence.
6. Here, our lives are forever impacted and changed, as was the case with the prophet Isaiah.
7. There is a distinct progression as we approach God's throne. That pathway leads us from the outer court, through the holy place, and into the holy of holies.

Devotional Exercises

#1 Progression

Take time in your personal devotions to explore choruses and hymns, as study guide questions 7 and 8 suggest. Try to become very familiar with the progression outlined in this chapter (outer court, holy place, and holy of holies), so you can pinpoint where you are at any given time along the pathway of praise and worship.

#2 Interaction

As you praise and worship during devotional times and church services, begin to pay closer attention to the messages of the songs and how they prompt you to interact with the Lord. Consider scriptures or biblical truths that come to mind as you meditate on the words and messages of various songs. During church services in particular, pay attention to how the message of one song fits with the next, and how a group of songs unveils an entire journey in the Lord's presence.

Study Guide Questions—Chapter 2

1. Explain what Hebrews 8:5 means when it indicates that the tabernacle of Moses was a shadow of the reality in heaven.
2. Considering what we learned about the tabernacle of Moses (the great importance God placed on all the details), how might God's attention to detail affect *our* praise and worship habits?
3. The heavenly reality depicted in Revelation chapter 4 is a very beautiful picture. Read it, then describe what you find most interesting and why.
4. Compare Matthew 27:51 and Hebrews 10:20.
    a) What is the significance of the temple curtain being torn from top to bottom?
    b) What does this have to do with our praise and worship today?
5. What does Psalm 22:3 mean—that God "inhabitest" our praise?
6. As you reflect on A. W. Tozer's comments, describe any experiences that you have had where you felt you were entering into a heavenly realm.
7. This lesson has talked about the pathway of praise and worship—from the outer court, through the holy place, and into the holy of holies. With this in mind, consider if the following songs would most appropriately be sung in the outer court, the holy place, or the holy of holies.

   "I Love You, Lord"
   "Again I Say Rejoice"
   "How Great Is Our God"
   "Let God Arise"

"Here I Am to Worship"
"He's All I Need"

8. We have come to understand praise and worship as a living interaction between God and His worshipers. With this in mind, consider the following songs and describe what might be happening in a person's heart as he or she is singing. Likewise, what might God be saying to the worshiper?

"I Surrender All"
All to Jesus, I surrender
All to Him I freely give
I will ever love and trust Him
In His presence daily live
I surrender all, I surrender all
All to Thee, my blessed Savior
I surrender all

Public Domain

"Give God the Glory"
Give God the glory
Give God the glory
Give God the glory
And He will give you the victory
Satan, the blood of Jesus is against you
Satan, the blood of Jesus is against you
Satan, the blood of Jesus is against you
So let us give God, so let us give God
So let us give God all of the praise

Copyright 1980 Butterfly Fuchsia Music Co.

"I Stand in Awe"

You are beautiful beyond description
Too marvelous for words
Too wonderful for comprehension
Like nothing ever seen or heard
Who can grasp Your infinite wisdom
Who can fathom the depth of Your love
You are beautiful beyond description
Majesty enthroned above
I stand, I stand in awe of You
I stand, I stand in awe of You
Holy God to Whom all praise is due
I stand in awe of You

Copyright 1987 Sovereign Grace Ministries

SET LIST EXERCISES

Directions:

1. For each set list provided, describe the interaction taking place between God and the worshiper.
2. Chart the progression, from the outer court, through the holy place, and into the holy of holies.

(Use a separate sheet of paper if necessary.)

Worship service
August 17, 2014

"Our God"
"Alive"
"Oceans"
"Waiting Here for You"
"I Love You, Lord"

"Our God"
Water You turned into wine, opened the eyes of the blind
There's no one like You, none like You
Into the darkness You shine, out of the ashes we rise
There's no one like You, none like You
Our God is greater, our God is stronger
God, You are higher than any other
Our God is healer, awesome in power, our God, our God
And if our God is for us, then who could ever stop us?
And if our God is with us, then what could stand against?
What could stand against?

Copyright 2010 Atlas Mountain Songs, sixsteps music, Thankyou Music, Vamos Publishing, and worshiptogether.com songs

"Alive"

I was lost with a broken heart
You picked me up, now I'm set apart
From the ash I am born again
Forever safe in the Savior's hands
You are more than my words could say
I'll follow You, Lord, for all my days
Fix my eyes, follow in Your ways
Forever free in unending grace
'Cause You are, You are, You are my freedom
We lift You higher, we lift You higher
Your love, Your love, Your love never-ending, oh, oh, oh
You are alive in us, nothing can take Your place
You are all we need, Your love has set us free, woh, woh

Copyright 2012 Hillsong Music Publishing

"Oceans"

You call me out upon the waters
The great unknown where feet may fail
And there I find You in the mystery
In oceans deep my faith will stand
And I will call upon Your name
And keep my eyes above the waves when oceans rise
My soul will rest in Your embrace
For I am Yours and You are mine
Spirit lead me where my trust is without borders
Let me walk upon the waters wherever You would call me
Take me deeper than my feet could ever wander
And my faith will be made stronger in the presence of my Savior

Copyright 2012 Hillsong Music Publishing

"Waiting Here for You"
If faith can move the mountains, let the mountains move
We come with expectation waiting here for You, waiting here for You
You're the Lord of all creation, and still You know my heart
The Author of salvation, You've loved us from the start
Waiting here for You with our hands lifted high in praise
And it's You we adore, singing alleluia
Singing alleluia, alleluia

Copyright 2011 Gloworks, sixsteps music, Vamos Publishing, and worshiptogether.com songs

"I Love You Lord"
I love You, Lord, and I lift my voice
To worship You, oh my soul rejoice
Take joy, my King, in what You hear
Let it be a sweet, sweet sound in Your ear

Copyright 1978 House of Mercy Music

Worship service
July 29, 2007

"Everyone (Praises)"
"Because of You"
"Freedom Reigns"
"King of All Kings"
"You Are Near"

"Everyone (Praises)"
Great in splendor, Lord of ev'rything
Worthy is Your name
Never-changing, ever-reigning King
Worthy is Your name
All creation rises up to declare Your wonders
As people ev'rywhere sing
Praises to the One Who saves us
Through His blood He gave us life
And now we come ev'ryone
Hallelujah, hallelujah

Copyright 2004 Integrity Music Publishing

"Because of You"

Never before have I felt so alive
Never before have I thought I could fly
Never before have I ever been so free
Being with You, I now begin to see
That Your presence overwhelms me
Because of You, I can dance
Because of You, I lift my hands
Because of You, I can sing, I am free
Never, never will I hold back again
Never, never will I go back again

Copyright 2003 CFN Music

"Freedom Reigns"

Where the Spirit of the Lord is, there is freedom
Where the Spirit of the Lord is, there is freedom
Freedom reigns in this place
Showers of mercy and grace
Falling on ev'ry face, there is freedom

Copyright 1998 Vineyard Music USA

"King of All Kings"

We rev'rence Your presence as we come into this holy place
Our eyes are on You now as we seek the beauty of Your face
So we come
To worship You, to honor You
To glorify Your Majesty
To worship You, to honor You
To glorify the King of all kings
You're brighter than the noonday sun
You're greater than our words can say
To Your kingdom there'll be no end
You are the High and Holy One
You reign upon Your throne
And for these reasons we come

Copyright 2005 Nichols Productions

"You Are Near"

In awe of You, we worship
And stand amazed at Your great love
We're changed from glory to glory
We set our hearts on You, our God
Now Your presence fills this place
Be exalted in our praise
As we worship, I believe You are near
Blessing and honor and glory and power
Forever, forever

Copyright 1999 Hillsong Music Publishing

Chapter 3

OUR ATTITUDE TOWARD PRAISE, WORSHIP, AND THE PRESENCE OF GOD

The attitude with which you come will determine the depth in which you go.

As established in chapters 1 and 2, a biblical understanding of praise and worship is crucial. Consideration of how we should approach the presence of God is likewise critical. Yet, we can have all the right information but not engage in biblical praise and worship. As chapter 3 will demonstrate, our *attitude* toward praise, worship, and the presence of God can be the determining factor between a fruitful life of victory and a barren life of defeat.

Let me expose an all-too-common misconception. Some Christians assume that because Christ made a way for us to enter in, we are automatically ushered into God's presence when we gather for times of praise and worship. An unintended result of this line of thinking is passivity in the average congregation. Let me explain.

If scripture tells me to live a holy life, and I know this is possible through God's righteousness and the Spirit's work, I am still faced with day-to-day decisions that will challenge my level of holiness. God's righteousness and the Spirit's work are essential, but they don't automatically shelter me from sin. In the same way, if scripture tells me to draw near to God, and I know this is possible through biblical praise and worship, I am nevertheless faced with a decision to enter in. I am not guaranteed an encounter with the Living God simply because the way has been opened for me.

> Hebrews 2:12: "He [Jesus] says, 'I will declare your name to my brothers; in the presence of the congregation I will sing your praises.'"

A lot of recent study has focused on the role of Jesus as our Chief Worship Leader. In Hebrews 2:12 to the right, we find that Jesus declares the Father's name among His brothers and sisters, and He sings the Father's praises in the congregation.

What follows is that the Father views our imperfect offerings of worship through the Son's perfect offering of worship, so our worship is acceptable because of what Christ has done and what Christ is doing during times of praise and worship, not because of anything we've done or anything we're doing. While this is more or less true, it could be misinterpreted as sitting back, relaxing, and letting Christ usher us in! I would propose that we have a great responsibility. True, we don't need to try and work something up in our own strength, but we don't need to sit by idly either.

Refusing to worship in our own strength does not mean we become passive. It simply means the pressure is taken off of our shoulders to somehow "pull out" a perfect offering. God is still looking for a sacrifice of praise and worship, and that will take effort on our part. *It is our choice.*

The fact that God left us with an ability to willfully make choices in this life is a general principle of His kingdom.

- Christ died for all, but we must *choose* to accept Him.
- Answers to prayer are provided, but we must *choose* to pray.
- There is truth in the Bible to resolve every plaguing question of faith and life, but we must *choose* to read it, study it, and hide it in our hearts.
- We may enter into the presence of Almighty God any time we desire because of the finished work of Christ on our behalf, but we must *choose* to enter.

It is difficult to understand why anyone would choose not to become a Christian, yet many do.

It is difficult to understand why believers facing a crisis choose to pull away from God by dropping church attendance, Bible reading, prayer, and fellowship with other believers, when this is the very time they need God's mercy, wisdom, help, and support of other believers. Yet many choose to pull away.

Similarly, it is difficult to understand why Christians, especially those in a free society who've been given access to the throne room of Almighty God *any time* they desire, would choose not to enter in!

- The way into His presence has been opened.
- The invitation has been offered. (See Psalm 100:4, Psalm 96:8, Revelation 22:17.)
- Nevertheless, the act of entering in must be a conscious, personal decision. It is *not* automatic but a choice of one's will.

Psalm 100:4: "Enter his gates with thanksgiving and his courts with praise; give thanks to him and praise his name."

Psalm 96:8: "Ascribe to the LORD the glory due his name; bring an offering and come into his courts."

Revelation 22:17: "The Spirit and the bride say, 'Come!' And let him who hears say, 'Come!' Whoever is thirsty, let him come; and whoever wishes, let him take the free gift of the water of life."

God is calling us to respond joyfully to the invitation. When we truly understand the *price* He paid to give us entry, and when we truly grasp the *awesome love* He has for us (which caused Him to pay that price in the first place), we will be filled with desire and anticipation for His courts.

When we truly comprehend the role biblical praise and worship plays as we enter in, we will feel as David did...

"Let us go to his dwelling place; let us worship at his footstool" (Psalm 132:7).

Attitudes toward Praise, Worship, and the Presence of God

If someone would approach you in the middle of the day and say, "Let's take thirty minutes and head into God's presence together," what would your first response be? "I'm too busy," "I'm not really thinking about God right now," "That's boring," or "*Yes*, I'd love to!"

The Cluttered Attitude

Read the following account, and make a mental note of what was going on…

"When it was almost time for the Jewish Passover, Jesus went up to Jerusalem. In the temple courts he found men selling cattle, sheep and doves, and others sitting at tables exchanging money. So he made a whip out of cords, and drove all from the temple area, both sheep and cattle; he scattered the coins of the money changers and overturned their tables. To those who sold doves he said, 'Get these out of here! How dare you turn my Father's house into a market!' His disciples remembered that it is written: 'Zeal for your house will consume me'" (John 2:13–17).

Consider this. Scores of people were hanging around the temple courts. And all of them were very busy. Yet, while some of them had attitudes of true devotion, Jesus, being moved with zeal (intense love) for the house of the Lord, saw many with *cluttered attitudes*—those who were consumed with things other than true devotion and desire to be in God's presence.

Animal keepers were there to make a sale, turn a profit, and/or protect their goods from thieves.

Others were there out of religious obligation. It was Jewish law and custom to come to the temple and offer sacrifices. It was something that had to be done.

Still others were there simply because they had nothing better to do, and they came to the temple to spend their time watching everyone else! They'd sit back on a ledge over in a corner and enjoy the hustling and bustling of activity, the doves fluttering about, and the sound of people conversing. They were consumed with/distracted by all that was taking place around them, instead of having a genuine desire for the presence of God.

I am sure, with some careful thought, you could come up with many other scenarios readily present on any given day in the temple courts. I'm also sure, without too much hesitation, you would discover some of these same scenarios in any worship gathering of any church, including yours! Maybe you've even seen yourself reflected in some of these scenarios.

The common denominator in all these situations is this: the people's lives were cluttered with things *other than the simple driving desire* to spend time in God's awesome presence. This should certainly challenge us, in this busy day and age, to prioritize His presence over other things.

The Heartless Attitude

Take a moment now and read some Old Testament accounts of rebellious Israelite attitudes in the book of Isaiah...

"When you come to appear before me, who has asked this of you, this trampling of my courts? Stop bringing meaningless offerings! Your incense is detestable to me. New Moons, Sabbaths and convocations—I cannot bear your evil assemblies" (Isaiah 1:12–13).

"The Lord says: 'These people come near to me with their mouth and honor me with their lips, but their hearts are far from me. Their worship of me is made up only of rules taught by men'" (Isaiah 29:13).

Sacrificial offerings of praise and worship had grown meaningless to the people of God. They had become, as we noticed earlier in John 2, only a matter of ritual and one's attempt to do what *should* be done. There was no longer any heart behind the practice, and the songs were meaningless noise in God's ear. Individuals would come to the temple, make sacrifices, and observe prescribed religious days and festivals, but the fire and meaning of these things had been snuffed out long before in the hearts of the people.

We sure see this attitude a lot in God's people today! They drag themselves out of bed after a weekend of fun (doing what they really enjoy), only to put their time in—to make an appearance. They sit (or maybe stand) through the praise and worship time, possibly mumbling some of the words to the songs, but in their hearts, they are painting the fence in the back yard, eyeing the crowd for that significant other, or wondering if the service will let out by noon.

Clearly, they are going through the motions. Their hearts are far from the Lord.

Yet, we often see others standing right beside the heartless ones, with intensity and passion on their faces, captivated by the Lord's presence!

The Conditional Attitude

This attitude says: "I will praise and worship God *if* circumstances are right. I will participate *if* life is going reasonably well... *if* you sing the songs I know and love... *if* you sing them in the style I prefer... *if* you sing them in the order I prefer... *if* you sing them at the volume I prefer... and *if* you do not ask me to participate in any way that would stretch me or violate my comfort zone... *then* I will participate."

Listen—participation in biblical praise and worship should *never* be dependent upon external circumstances such as type of song, what instruments are being used, who is leading, who's standing next to me, order of the service, whether circumstances of my life are rosy or falling apart at the seams, whether I feel happy or sad at the given moment, etc.

Praise and worship is first and foremost validated by *who God is* (which never changes)...

"Every good and perfect gift is from above, coming down from the Father of the heavenly lights, who does not change like shifting shadows" (James 1:17).

It's validated by His unconditional love for us (from which we can never be separated)...

"For I am convinced that neither death nor life, neither angels nor demons, neither the present nor the future, nor any powers, neither height nor depth, nor anything else in all creation, will be able to separate us from the love of God that is in Christ Jesus our Lord" (Romans 8:38–39).

And it's validated by what He has already accomplished for us through His completed work on the cross (which can never be defeated)...

"For you know that it was not with perishable things such as silver or gold that you were redeemed from the empty way of life handed down to you from your forefathers, but with the precious blood of Christ, a Lamb without blemish or defect" (1 Peter 1:18–19).

Our God is eternal, almighty, ever-present, all-knowing, and holy! And He's done great things for us! So He is worthy of our praise, regardless of how we feel.

Even when we're struggling spiritually, that doesn't mean we cease to worship Him. Many Christians have somehow come to the conclusion that they can't approach God in praise and worship unless they've first been purified. But God never said that! If anything, He demonstrates quite the opposite. The sinful woman in Luke 7, for instance, worshiped first; then she was purified. Let's come into God's presence, not based on how good we are but, instead, on how good *God* is.

Let's refuse to be in bondage to a conditional attitude. Let's freely enter in through heartfelt praise and worship at all times! (This was certainly the example of the prophet Habakkuk and the psalmists, as seen in Habakkuk 3:17–18 and Psalm 34:1, 61:8, 63:4, & 71:14.)

Habakkuk 3:17–18: "Though the fig tree does not bud and there are no grapes on the vines, though the olive crop fails and the fields produce no food, though there are no sheep in the pen and no cattle in the stalls, yet I will rejoice in the LORD, I will be joyful in God my Savior."

Psalm 34:1: "Of David. When he pretended to be insane before Abimelech, who drove him away, and he left. I will extol the LORD at all times; his praise will always be on my lips."

Psalm 61:8: "I ever sing praise to your name and fulfill my vows day after day."

Psalm 63:4: "I will praise you as long as I live, and in your name I will lift up my hands."

Psalm 71:14: "But as for me, I will always have hope; I will praise you more and more."

The Complacent Attitude

This attitude treats His presence as no big deal. It's a "take it or leave it" approach.

Complacent people are not filled with gratitude for opportunities to worship God, *or* they fail to realize the awesome privilege of entering in.

I believe the contemporary church by and large has developed a concert mentality when it comes to corporate praise and worship, and this has produced a lot of complacency. Auditorium seats face forward, like a performance venue, and individuals "perform" on a stage, while the "audience" casually observes.

Please know that I highly value approaches to praise and worship that make sense in today's culture. But if our services begin to resemble concerts more than a living interaction with God, people will automatically pass such experiences through the concert filter, and we will have more spectators than participants in the room. Leadership must make the point (and make it often) that praise and worship is not a concert; otherwise, the crowd will simply watch a performance on a stage.

Complacency is a *big problem* in today's church (especially the Western church), and God has a lot to say in His Word about it. In fact, He spoke a very strong message about complacent attitudes through the prophet Malachi…

"'A son honors his father, and a servant his master. If I am a father, where is the honor due me? If I am a master, where is the respect due me?' says the LORD Almighty. 'It is you, O priests, who show contempt for my name. But you ask, "How have we shown contempt for your name?" You place defiled food on my altar. But you ask, "How have we defiled you?" By saying that the Lord's table is contemptible. When you bring blind animals for sacrifice, is that not wrong? When you sacrifice crippled or diseased animals, is that not wrong? Try offering them to your governor! Would he be pleased with you? Would he accept you?' says the LORD Almighty. 'Now implore God to be gracious to us. With such offerings from your hands, will he accept you?'—says the LORD Almighty" (Malachi 1:6–9).

Here's the context. The people of God had developed an attitude of complacency, demonstrated in the lowering of their sacrificial standards. Each animal was supposed to be a healthy, spotless lamb—the *best* from the flock. But by sacrificing less than one's best, the people were demonstrating their lack of concern for the Lord and His presence. Here, God was finally calling them on the carpet. He accused them of bringing substandard sacrifices, since the diseased and dying lambs they were offering would probably die anyway. The Lord reminded them that they wouldn't even present something this pitiful to their earthly leaders. Why, then, would they even think about presenting it to Almighty God?

It was bad enough that they sacrificed such animals, but notice the extent of their attitude. In verse 7, God exposed the underlying problem, saying, "The Lord's table (or presence) is contemptible"—that is, common, or not worthy of much consideration. Furthermore, notice their *expectation* in verse 9. They would bring the polluted sacrifices to the temple and command the priests to tell God to bless them, saying, "We've done what He has asked!"

Later, God gave a terrifying warning to these priests. Read it in the Living Bible…

"If you don't change your ways and give glory to my name, then I will send terrible punishment upon you, and instead of giving you blessings as I would like to, I will turn on you with curses. Indeed, I have cursed you already because you haven't taken seriously the things that are most important to me" (Malachi 2:1).

Romans 12:1: "Therefore, I urge you, brothers, in view of God's mercy, to offer your bodies as living sacrifices, holy and pleasing to God—this is your spiritual act of worship."

1 Peter 2:5, 9: "You also, like living stones, are being built into a spiritual house to be a holy priesthood, offering spiritual sacrifices acceptable to God through Jesus Christ … but you are a chosen people, a royal priesthood, a holy nation, a people belonging to God, that you may declare the praises of him who called you out of darkness into his wonderful light."

Hebrews 13:15: "Through Jesus, therefore, let us continually offer to God a sacrifice of praise—the fruit of lips that confess his name."

Remember, as New Testament believers, *we* are now God's priests, and it is *our* privilege and responsibility to offer sacrifices to God (not lambs and goats, but our lives and our gifts of praise and worship). (See Romans 12:1; 1 Peter 2:5, 9; Hebrews 13:15.)

Question—Have you ever been guilty of offering praise and worship that was less than your best? Of course. We all have. Most of us don't intend to be complacent, but this attitude creeps into our lives ever so subtly. Maybe we need to confess the sin of complacency. Maybe it's as simple as feeding on His presence more, so we develop a healthy appetite for it.

The Despising Attitude

A despising attitude goes beyond complacency and becomes hardened, bitter, and judgmental. It is this attitude that motivates some during praise and worship to fold their arms, set their jaw, and think to themselves, "Look at how foolish this is… I'm not going to participate in this… These people are making imbeciles out of themselves… Why, I'm embarrassed to even be around them!"

This was the attitude that King David's wife exhibited as he (a worshiper after God's own heart) was dancing and celebrating in the streets of Jerusalem when the Ark of the Lord's Presence was being returned to the city…

> David, wearing a linen ephod, danced before the LORD with all his might, while he and the entire house of Israel brought up the ark of the LORD with shouts and the sound of trumpets. As the ark of the LORD was entering the City of David, Michal daughter of Saul watched from a window. And when she saw King David leaping and dancing before the LORD, she despised him in her heart … When David returned home to bless his household, Michal daughter of Saul came out to meet him and said, "How the king of Israel has distinguished himself today, disrobing in the sight of the slave girls of his servants as any vulgar fellow would!" David said to Michal, "It was before the LORD, who chose me rather than your father or anyone from his house when he appointed me ruler over the Lord's people Israel—I will celebrate before the LORD. I will become even more undignified than this, and I will be humiliated in my own eyes. But by these slave girls you spoke of, I will be held in honor." And Michal daughter of Saul had no children to the day of her death (2 Samuel 6:14–16, 20–23).

(Incidentally, this was the same ark that had been in the holy of holies, in the tabernacle of Moses, above which were the golden cherubim.)

We must understand that praise and worship does not have to be acceptable to *us* but, rather, to *God*. It is His praise, not ours! We must never allow ourselves to develop a despising, judgmental attitude toward others as they express themselves in praise and worship. In a corporate setting, any expression that's in order and within biblical parameters is acceptable to God, if presented out of a sincere heart. Furthermore, if something is expressed that you feel is *not* within biblical parameters, or you feel may be out of order, remember, it is not your place to judge, but it is the responsibility of the pastor or overseer of the meeting. You should be caught up with your own expressions of devotion. We will deal in more detail with specific expressions of praise and worship and their appropriateness, as well as the leadership and administration of the Holy Spirit during corporate times of praise and worship, in later chapters. But for now, suffice it to say that praise and worship belongs to Him, and we should be more concerned with *our attitude* than *other people's expression.*

Notice the seriousness of the consequences visited upon Michal (verse 23): barrenness. I truly believe that many Christians today are spiritually barren—fruitless because of the despising attitudes they have nurtured in their hearts concerning praise and worship. This unhealthy attitude has been like a cancer, destroying these people from the inside out. The idea at least warrants some consideration.

David's Attitude toward Praise and Worship

Now let's move toward the conclusion of this chapter by exploring David's attitude toward praise and worship. He is a worthy example, having been called a man after God's own heart. Before he was a king or warrior, David was a worshiper. He not only organized a system of musical worship for the house of God, but he modeled expressions that moved the nation of Israel to higher levels of praise and worship.

For instance, David demonstrated childlike humility as he danced before the Lord. This surely inspired many people to follow his lead in offering uninhibited praise to God.

Furthermore, our ultimate role model, *Jesus*, showed us how to worship the Father through heartfelt praise and worship. Remember, it was Jesus who said that we must become like little children. (See Luke 18:16–17.)

> Luke 18:16–17: "But Jesus called the children to him and said, 'Let the little children come to me, and do not hinder them, for the kingdom of God belongs to such as these. I tell you the truth, anyone who will not receive the kingdom of God like a little child will never enter it.'"

They were the ones caught up praising the Son of God at His triumphal entry into Jerusalem, as depicted in Matthew and Luke…

"But when the chief priests and the teachers of the law saw the wonderful things he did and the children shouting in the temple area, 'Hosanna to the Son of David,' they were indignant. 'Do you hear what these children are saying?' they asked him. 'Yes,' replied Jesus, 'have you never read, "From the lips of children and infants you have ordained praise"?'" (Matthew 21:15–16).

"The whole crowd of disciples began joyfully to praise God in loud voices for all the miracles they had seen: 'Blessed is the king who comes in the name of the Lord! Peace in heaven and glory in the highest!' Some of the Pharisees in the crowd said to Jesus, 'Teacher, rebuke your disciples!' 'I tell you,' he replied, 'if they keep quiet, the stones will cry out'" (Luke 19:37–40).

It was the dignified, religious people who had a problem with this sort of behavior. Consider the fact that if this kind of praise was unacceptable and irreverent, Jesus had the perfect opportunity to squelch it. Instead, He commended the kids and told the religious, stuffy folks (in different words) that the rocks have more sense than you!

Even the most common Hebrew word for "praise" in our English Bible depicts an exuberant show of emotion lavished upon God. The word is *halal*, from which we get our English word *hallelujah*. If you study the Hebrew meaning of this word, you'll find that it actually means to do what Michal thought was inappropriate—to make a show, to be hilarious or clamorously foolish, to rave or boast!

Please understand, such show of emotion is not displayed for our own enjoyment or to draw attention to ourselves, but because God is extremely worthy and deserving of our absolute best. This is what David meant when he said in Psalm 103:1…

"Praise the LORD, O my soul; all my inmost being, *praise his holy name*" (emphasis added).

David's attitude (and better yet, Jesus's attitude) toward praise, worship, and God's presence was one of absolute devotion, overwhelming passion, childlike humility, and sincere anticipation!

This attitude must also be ours.

Food for thought as we close: Through worship, I determine who I'm going to be. Would I rather be religious and stuffy, or genuine and passionate?

Summation

1. We may enter into the presence of Almighty God any time we desire because of the finished work of Christ on our behalf, but we must always *choose* to enter.
2. The person with a cluttered attitude fills his or her life with things other than the simple driving desire to be in God's presence.
3. The person with a heartless attitude may be going through the motions during praise and worship, but there is no passion or depth of meaning.
4. The person with a conditional attitude participates in praise and worship (or not) depending on whether certain external circumstances are present rather than focusing on the consistency of who God is, His unconditional love for us, and what He has accomplished on our behalf.
5. The person with a complacent attitude views God's presence as common; this person devalues his or her privilege to enter in, and there is willingness to give God less than one's best in praising and worshiping the Lord.

6. The person with a despising attitude allows himself or herself to become hardened, bitter, and judgmental as he or she views others' worship of God.
7. David's attitude toward praise, worship, and the courts of the Lord was one of absolute devotion, overwhelming passion, childlike humility, and sincere anticipation.

Devotional Exercises

1. Monitor your attitudes closely this week during personal devotional times and corporate worship times. Note what is revealed. Consider what factors may be hindering you. Is there something you can do, or a way you can adjust your thinking, to avoid negative attitudes?
2. Take a moment after the next corporate worship service and jot some brief notes on a piece of paper. Note things such as:
    - Progressions or themes you sensed
    - What God was affirming to you
    - Your attitude and/or countenance

Study Guide Questions—Chapter 3

1. Why might you choose *not* to enter into God's presence, and how might you address this?
2. Of all the negative attitudes, which one do you find yourself slipping into most? (Be encouraged! The majority of us fall prey to several of them more often than we desire.) What practical things can you (or others around you) do to help you overcome this particular attitude?
3. What is the most difficult circumstance you encounter when entering into praise and worship (life, others around you, musical distractions, etc.)? Give some suggestions as to how you might overcome this difficulty.
4. Give several examples of how a New Testament believer might bring substandard spiritual sacrifices to the Lord in times of praise and worship. (Please remember, *you* are not

substandard! You're made righteous through the blood of Jesus!)

5. When you consider the account of David and his wife, Michal, what insights come to your mind?
6. What do you appreciate most about David's attitude toward God's presence? What do you find most challenging?
7. Out of the first three lessons, what has been the most powerful thing you have learned?

Chapter 4

THE INTIMACY AND FRUIT OF OUR PRAISE AND WORSHIP

Introduction

Chapters 1–3 have begun to lay a clear biblical foundation for New Testament praise and worship. So far, we have learned that:

1. The substitutionary sacrifice of Jesus Christ on our behalf has cleansed us from sin and enabled us to enter into the immediate presence of God—with confidence.
2. As believers, we understand that God's Spirit is in us, and His presence is all around us. But there is a distinct progression we follow as we endeavor to draw near to His *manifest* presence.
3. Praise and worship (and also prayer) is the primary vehicle that carries us along this pathway, allowing us to become increasingly aware of His habitation.
4. As we pass from the outer court, through the holy place, and into a holy of holies encounter with God, we recognize that He is enthroned in our midst. We are aware that He is seated among us.

5. Thus, as we find ourselves in this heavenly throne room, where the glorified Christ is seated, we engage in a living interaction with the Lord.
6. Finally, we learned in the previous chapter that we must always *choose* to enter in, and the attitude with which we come will determine the depth in which we go.

At this point, we can dive into chapter 4. While the first three chapters have dealt with the progression and the pathway that will take us into God's presence, this lesson will focus on what happens to us once we're in the manifest presence of God. It will further define the living interaction.

The Relationship between Old and New Testaments

Clearly seen in the first few chapters, there is a direct relationship between Old and New Testaments. This link is highly significant for all New Testament believers…

"The law is only a shadow of the good things that are coming—not the realities themselves" (Hebrews 10:1).

The old covenant was given to Moses on the mountain after the Israelites came out of Egypt. It was a type of contract between God and His people, as outlined in the law and commandments.

As we see in the New Testament, this old covenant pointed to a time when God would be more intimate with His people. Before this was possible, however, sinful man needed the work of Christ to deal with the barrier of sin. We know that this was accomplished through the suffering, death, and resurrection of Jesus, and a new covenant was subsequently initiated. Take a moment and read what the book of Hebrews says regarding a key difference in the degree of intimacy between God and His people from old to new covenants. Keep in mind that we, as New Testament believers, are part of the new and living covenant…

"But God found fault with the people and said: 'The time is coming,' declares the Lord, 'when I will make a new covenant with the house of Israel and with the house of Judah. It will not be like the covenant I made with their forefathers when I took them by the hand to lead them out of Egypt, because they did not remain faithful to my covenant, and I turned away from them,' declares the Lord. 'This is the covenant I will make with the house of Israel after that time,' declares the Lord. 'I will put my laws in their minds and write them on their hearts. I will be their God, and they will be my people. No longer will a man teach his neighbor, or a man his brother, saying, "*Know* the Lord," because they will all *know* me, from the least of them to the greatest. For I will forgive their wickedness and will remember their sins no more'" (Hebrews 8:8–12, emphasis added).

To fully appreciate what is being said here, a simple Greek word study is in order. In verse 11 of Hebrews chapter 8, the first time "know" appears, it is the Greek word *ginosko*, which means "to have knowledge of; to perceive, feel or be aware of."[7] It is *knowing* in the general sense.

However, the second time "know" appears in verse 11, it is a different Greek word altogether. It's the word *eido*, which means "to know; to perceive or be aware of as a result of having beheld or looked upon in a face-to-face experience!"[8] In other words, (actually, in *real* words), the writer to the Hebrews is saying to the people of the new covenant (including us), "You won't have to say to each other 'know' (get general knowledge of) the Lord, because we will all 'know' Him by enjoying the intimacy of a face-to-face relationship with Him!"

Now compare this truth with what you've learned about the veil separating us from God's immediate presence, and how praise and worship brings us close to Him and His throne! *A face-to-face relationship is a genuine part of our living interaction!* But it gets even better.

---

[7] *Ginosko* (Strong's *Gk1097*) as defined in *A Concise Dictionary of the Words in the Greek Testament with Their Renderings in the Authorized English Version* (Nashville, TN: Abingdon Press, 1973), 20.

[8] *Eido* (Strong's *Gk1492*) as defined in *A Concise Dictionary of the Words in the Greek Testament with Their Renderings in the Authorized English Version* (Nashville, TN: Abingdon Press, 1973), 25; and as expounded upon in *MacLaren's Commentary* (Exposition of Holy Scripture), by Alexander MacLaren.

Isaiah 62:5: "As a young man marries a maiden, so will your sons marry you; as a bridegroom rejoices over his bride, so will your God rejoice over you."

Jeremiah 2:2: "Go and proclaim in the hearing of Jerusalem: 'I remember the devotion of your youth, how as a bride you loved me and followed me through the desert, through a land not sown.'"

Revelation 19:7: "Let us rejoice and be glad and give him glory! For the wedding of the Lamb has come, and his bride has made herself ready."

Revelation 21:9–10: "One of the seven angels ... said to me, 'Come, I will show you the bride, the wife of the Lamb.' And he carried me away in the Spirit to a mountain great and high, and showed me the Holy City, Jerusalem, coming down out of heaven from God."

New Testament Believers: The Bride of Christ

The fact that we (New Testament believers) are the Bride of Christ and Jesus is our Bridegroom is clearly portrayed in scripture and is a widely accepted principle among Bible scholars of nearly every persuasion. (Consider the scriptures to the left: Isaiah 62:5, Jeremiah 2:2, Revelation 19:7 and 21:9–10.)

The *Christ-Centered Exposition Commentary* goes on to say:

"The use of the marriage metaphor to describe the relationship of God to His people is almost universal in scripture. From the time that God chose Israel to be His own in the Sinai Desert, the covenant was pictured in terms of a marriage. Idolatry was equated with adultery (Exodus 34:10–17). Yahweh is a jealous God (in a loving, not overbearing sense). Monogamous marriage is the norm for depicting the covenant relationship throughout Scripture, climaxing with the Marriage Supper of the Lamb. God has chosen a bride."[9]

(For an interesting comparative study of the New Testament "reality" of the Bride of Christ and the Old Testament "shadow" of the Jewish wedding, see the pages directly following the study guide questions at the close of this chapter.)

Bridal Intimacy and Its Fruit

So what does all of this have to do with praise and worship? Much, in every way! Keep reading.

Consider the prophet Daniel, as he is speaking to the people

[9] Daniel L. Akin, "Exalting Jesus in Song of Songs" from *The Christ-Centered Exposition Commentary Series* (Nashville, TN: B&H Publishing, 2015), 5.

of God concerning the effect their enemies would have on them. Look at the King James *and* New International Versions to the right (Daniel 11:32).

> Daniel 11:32 (KJV): "And such as do wickedly against the covenant shall he corrupt by flatteries: but the people that do *know* their God shall be strong, and do exploits" (emphasis added).
>
> Daniel 11:32 (NIV): "With flattery he will corrupt those who have violated the covenant, but the people who *know* their God will firmly resist him" (emphasis added).

It seems that the ability of God's people to stand against their enemies, to be strong and do exploits, has something to do with them knowing Him. But there's more.

In this instance, "know" appears in the original language as *yada*,[10] and it's the exact same word used in Genesis 4:1. Read this to the right in the King James Version, then compare the NIV's rendering. (While it is true that *yada* is used 944 times in scripture, and the word has varying shades or degrees of meaning, it is quite clear that knowing God is connected with intimacy, and the exchange between the Lord and His worshipers gives birth to something fruitful. So we're not only talking about a living interaction or face-to-face relationship, but also a life-producing exchange!)

> Genesis 4:1 (KJV): "And Adam *knew* Eve his wife; and she *conceived*, and bore Cain, and said, 'I have gotten a man from the LORD'" (emphasis added).
>
> Genesis 4:1 (NIV): "Adam *lay with* his wife Eve, and she *became pregnant* and gave birth to Cain. She said, 'With the help of the LORD I have brought forth a man'" (emphasis added).

Now, I know what you're thinking. And I'm not intending to equate our devotional acts of praise and worship with sexual relations between a man and a woman. Keep in mind, though, that spiritual intimacy between God and His covenant people is actually the *perfect reality* from which God patterned the intimacy of sexual relations.

He provided the shadow for husbands and wives, as one of the

---

[10] *Yada* (Strong's Hb3045) as defined in *A Concise Dictionary of the Words in the Hebrew Bible with Their Renderings in the Authorized English Version* (Nashville, TN: Abingdon Press, 1973), 47.

most powerful expressions of deep and intimate love within the covenant of marriage. Yet, there is a purer, stronger, more fulfilling, life-giving exchange between Christ, the heavenly Bridegroom, and the church, His blood-bought Bride. (Compare what is being said here to what you have learned in prior lessons concerning the *shadow* on earth and the *reality* in heaven.)

Men, this is harder for us. Even as I'm engaging in this study and writing these thoughts, I feel a little awkward, and my mind continually tries to pull me into the *shadow* and not the *reality*. Let me be blunt. We are not "making out" with the Lord during times of praise and worship! To come to that conclusion is to interpret the *perfect reality* in light of the *imperfect shadow*. If it helps, compare this God-and-you intimacy with the best example you've seen of an earthly father loving his son, and I'd say that's a starting point (though pale in comparison to the Lord's love for His sons).

The Fruit of Our Praise and Worship

To gain a richer understanding of the thoughts explored above, we must consider the following point. This intimacy is more than emotional intensity or passionate experience. It is *life-giving*. It is *fruitful!* Read Genesis 4:1 again on the previous page. There was conception. The NIV says she became pregnant as a result of this intimacy of knowing. Furthermore, the life conceived within this bride was nurtured and cared for in her womb until the established time of delivery. When the time arrived, (having little to do with the will of the woman), the labor pains began and, with the bride's cooperation, the life that had been conceived within her during intimate relations was finally birthed into physical reality.

Here's the point. We, as Christ's Bride, have the privilege and responsibility of coming into an intimate, living interaction with Him through praise, worship, and prayer, whereby new life is conceived within the womb of our hearts.

This new life can be several things. Maybe it's encouragement from God or a physical healing. Maybe it's renewal of your mind in a certain area or removal of an addiction such as smoking or pornography. Maybe it's freedom from the bondage of anger. It might be the promise of a loved one's salvation or the hope that something beautiful is about to come to pass in your own life. This conception of new life could even be the deposit of a call to lay ministry or full-time pastoral work.

Whatever form this new life takes, the point is this: when we as the Bride of Christ enter into life-giving intimacy with God through biblical praise, worship, and prayer, *something* of God is deposited/conceived in the womb of our hearts. If nurtured and cared for through persistent relationship with Him, this "seed" continues to grow and develop within us until a divinely set time, when it has matured to the point of being birthed. Through a cooperative process, something finally comes to pass, and, as in the case of Genesis 4:1, that thing is from the Lord!

The Role of Intercessory Prayer

I believe this picture helps illustrate the role of intercessory prayer on the part of the Body (Bride) of Christ. Jesus taught us to pray, "Thy kingdom come on earth as it is in heaven." Are we willing to be agents of prayer, called to nurture the will of God in this earth?

We see several pictures of the birthing prayer in scripture. It is usually referred to as the "prayer of travail."

In Galatians 4:19 (to the right), Paul described himself as a mother who went through the pains of childbirth to see the Galatians' conversion and growth in Christ come to pass, and he was seemingly in labor once again as a result of the Galatians' apparent defection from the gospel.

> Galatians 4:19: "My dear children, for whom I am again in the pains of childbirth until Christ is formed in you,"
>
> James 5:16–18: "The prayer of a righteous man is powerful and effective. Elijah was a man just like us. He prayed earnestly that it would not rain, and it did not rain on the land for three and a half years. Again he prayed, and the heavens gave rain, and the earth produced its crops."

In James 5:16–18, the brother of Jesus says, in essence, "If you want to see an example of prayer that accomplishes much, consider the Prophet Elijah, specifically when he prayed for drought and then rain." (See the NIV translation to the right.) This is a direct citation of 1 Kings 18:42–45, where Elijah assumed the physical posture of a woman in travail, about to give birth—and he prayed seven times that the heavens would produce rain. Finally, there appeared a cloud the size of a man's hand that quickly grew to fill the sky and poured an abundance of rain on the drought-ravaged nation.

Conclusion

Could it be that during those intimate moments of worship, we (the people of God, the Bride of Christ) are "impregnated" with this divine seed that we must carry and nurture in the womb of our hearts, allowing it to grow and develop until God, through the Holy Spirit, moves us into the "delivery room," and in moments and days and months, through a willing cooperation with the Holy Spirit, through the labor of persistent prayer, God births what was once a small seed into a glorious physical reality? Let me say a resounding *yes*!

So how does this affect our approach toward praise and worship? It should *revolutionize* the experience!

We have indeed adopted a very dwarfed and limited view of praise and worship when we see it simply as a few warm-up songs before the sermon! The experience we've described above is not only fruitful in the sense that God has brought new life, but there's also been a deepening of the relationship. And this often has a profound effect on all of our other relationships. When we are truly experiencing God's life-giving, fruit-bearing presence, we will develop His heart for those around us and will want to serve them with love and compassion. Clearly, there's a lot at stake here.

I believe that as we truly come to an understanding of what God is trying to accomplish during times of praise and worship, we will never be the same, and we will never again be satisfied with superficial praise and worship! Let's cultivate spiritual receptivity.

In closing, let me make one final observation. It is often said that praise and worship is all about Him—that our focus should be on Him and Him alone. The previous lesson even suggested that we must have a "giving" rather than "getting" mentality when we worship. But clearly, *we benefit* and *others benefit around us* when we engage in biblical praise and worship. True, we should make Him the primary focus of our devotion, but as we do, He sees to it that we (and others) are blessed.

Summation

1. Hebrews 8:8–12 confirms that under the new covenant, God was going to have a more intimate, face-to-face relationship with His people. All New Testament believers are part of this new and living covenant.
2. Furthermore, we (New Testament believers) are the Bride of Christ, and Jesus is our Bridegroom, as outlined in the scriptures.
3. The highest degree of intimacy between a man and his wife is a type of the perfect intimacy we enjoy as the Bride of Christ in praise, worship, and prayer, though it pales in comparison to the life-giving exchange between Christ, the heavenly Bridegroom, and His church, the blood-bought Bride.
4. This high level of intimacy is life-giving, in that our intimate encounter with the presence of God produces a divine seed within the womb of our hearts.
5. This divine seed comes in a variety of forms, such as a promise from God, a physical touch in body, a supernatural deliverance, or even a call to ministry.
6. As the Bride of Christ, we then have the responsibility to carry this seed of life to full term through spiritual nurture and prayer, until the appointed time for the thing to be birthed into physical reality.
7. When we draw near to the delivery room, we may experience birthing pains as we enter into a time of intense travail or intercession.

Devotional Exercise

Pick a particular seed that God has deposited in your heart and make note of any progress or setback you experience during the remaining weeks of this study. It will be interesting to see how the seed matures, and whether it is birthed into reality over the next several weeks!

Study Guide Questions—Chapter 4

1. In your own words, explain the difference between the level of intimacy available to those under the old covenant versus those under the new and living covenant.
2. As you consider the fact that you are part of the Bride of Christ, how does this realization affect your worship, in terms of intimacy?
3. Think back over the years. What are some examples of God impregnating your heart with seeds of hope or seeds of life?
4. In the above examples, how long did you carry these seeds until they were actually birthed into reality?
5. Which seeds are you still nurturing in the womb of your heart?
6. How might you continue to nurture these premature deposits of life?
7. What was the most important thing you learned in this lesson?

The table below illustrates similarities between the New Testament "reality" of the Bride of Christ and the Old Testament "shadow" of the Jewish wedding.

THE JEWISH WEDDING	RELATIONSHIP TO NEW TESTAMENT LIFE
1. The prospective bridegroom took the initiative and traveled from his father's house to the home of the bride.	**Christ left His Father's house and came to earth to gain a bride for Himself.** John 1:14 "The word became flesh and made His dwelling among us. We have seen His glory, the glory of the One and Only, who came from the Father, full of grace and truth."
2. The father of the bride negotiated with the prospective bridegroom, coming up with a purchase price for his daughter. (Payment was solely the groom's responsibility.)	**Christ had to pay the price with His own blood.** I Corinthians 6:19-20 "Do you know that your body is a temple of the Holy Spirit, who is in you, whom you have received from God? You are not your own; you were bought at a price. Therefore honor God with your body."
3. When the groom paid the purchase price, the marriage covenant was established. At that point, the man and woman were thought to be husband and wife, even though no physical union had taken place.	**Through Christ's blood, the believer has been sanctified, or set apart, for the Lord's purposes.** Ephesians 5:25-27 "Husbands, love your wives, just as Christ loved the church and gave himself up for her to make her holy, cleansing her by the washing with water through the word, and to present her to himself as a radiant church, without stain or wrinkle or any other blemish, but holy and blameless."
4. After the covenant had been established, the bride and groom drank from a cup, over which the engagement benediction was pronounced. This sealed the covenant relationship.	**This marriage covenant was symbolized through communion at the Last Supper, as a new and living covenant was established between Christ and His Church.** I Corinthians 11:25 "In the same way, after supper he took the cup, saying, 'This cup is the new covenant in my blood; do this, whenever you drink it, in remembrance of me.'"

THE JEWISH WEDDING	RELATIONSHIP TO NEW TESTAMENT LIFE
5. After the marriage covenant went into effect, the groom left the home of the bride and returned to his father's house. He remained there for a period of twelve months, separated from his bride.	**Christ returned to His Father's house, following His substitutionary death and resurrection.** Acts 1:7-9 "He said to them: 'It is not for you to know the times or dates the Father has set by his own authority. But you will receive power when the Holy Spirit comes on you; and you will be my witnesses in Jerusalem, and in all Judea and Samaria, and to the ends of the earth.' After he said this, he was taken up before their very eyes, and a cloud hid him from their sight."
6. During this period of separation: **a. The groom prepared living accommodations for the bride, in his father's house.** **b. The bride gathered her wardrobe and prepared for married life.**	**Christ is preparing a place for His Bride, and God has sent pastors and teachers to perfect the Bride for the coming wedding.** **a)** John 14:2 "In my Father's house are many rooms; if it were not so, I would have told you. I am going there to prepare a place for you." **b)** Ephesians 4:11-13 "It was he who gave some to be apostles, some to be prophets, some to be evangelists, and some to be pastors and teachers, to prepare God's people for works of service, so that the body of Christ may be built up until we all reach unity in the faith and in the knowledge of the Son of God and become mature, attaining to the whole measure of the fullness of Christ."
7. After this period of separation, the groom, best man, and other male escorts left the house of the groom's father, usually at night, and conducted a torch-led procession to the house of the bride.	**Christ will soon come from His Father's house in heaven, accompanied by an angelic host.** John 14:3 "And if I go and prepare a place for you, I will come back and take you to be with me that you also may be where I am."
8. The bride was expecting her groom to come for her; however, she did not know the exact time. Thus, the groom's arrival was preceded by a shout.	**Christ's return will be preceded by a shout. We expect His coming, but we do not know the day or the hour.** I Thesselonians 4:16 "For the Lord himself will come down from heaven, with a loud command, with the voice of the archangel and with the trumpet call of God, and the dead in Christ shall rise first."

[11] Material adapted from "Betrothal," "Marriage," "Marriage Ceremonies," and "Marriage Laws" of The Jewish Encyclopedia: A Descriptive Record of the History, Religion, Literature, and Customs of the Jewish People from Earliest Times (New York: Funk and Wagnalls, 1901). Public domain.

Chapter 5

THE PATHWAY OF PRAISE: WORSHIPING IN SPIRIT

Once we understand our access into the presence of God through genuine praise and worship, we must realize that entering in is not the *end* but, rather, the *beginning.*

In chapter 4, we further defined the living interaction of praise and worship. We discovered that when we enter into His intimate presence as the Bride of Christ, divine seeds of life, hope, or calling are deposited in the womb of our hearts, and these seeds are carefully nurtured through persistent prayer and continuous feeding on God's Word. As the seeds mature within us, and we approach the God-appointed time that something will be birthed into physical reality, we may be led into intense seasons of prayer—sometimes lasting minutes, but often lasting weeks, months, or even years.

Also in previous chapters, we've discussed the progression of praise and worship from the outer court, through the holy place, and into a holy of holies encounter with God. One should keep in mind that this progression is not always clearly defined and should not be viewed as a rigid construct. For example, changing the tempo or personalizing the words of an outer court song may make it entirely suitable for the inner courts. And whether or not we're actually having a holy of holies encounter with God largely depends on where the congregation is as a whole. Just because we are singing a more intimate song does not somehow guarantee that we will be worshiping in an intimate place. If there is a major distraction in the service, or the people have not adequately prepared their hearts for worship, discouragement or heaviness can simply be carried into what's intended to be an intimate holy of holies time with the Lord.

That being said, the progression of praise and worship is generally depicted as moving from less intimate songs of praise to more intimate songs of worship.

With this foundation in place, we will discuss in this chapter how the progression of praise and worship continues, even once we've reached the holy of holies. Once we're in the manifest presence of God, the journey continues as we find ourselves being led by the Holy Spirit down different pathways to accomplish different purposes that the Spirit is orchestrating. Corporately, this can happen on a small or large scale, as the Holy Spirit leads a small group of people or an entire congregation down a particular path.

It is through our understanding and perception of these different pathways that praise and worship will take on a new, multifaceted dimension. The things we are about to discover will transform every praise and worship experience into a unique, dynamic adventure with God, whether individual or corporate.

Later, I want to identify a few well-traveled pathways for the sake of illustration and for the purpose of teaching some general maneuvering skills as you progress along your particular worship journey. Keep in mind, though, that there are no limitations to the type and number of pathways you may find yourself traveling during any praise and worship experience.

The Kind of Praise and Worship the Father Seeks

Please take a moment to read the passage below, which serves as a foundational scripture for the next several lessons…

> The Pharisees heard that Jesus was gaining and baptizing more disciples than John, although in fact it was not Jesus who baptized, but his disciples. When the Lord learned of this, he left Judea and went back

once more to Galilee. Now he had to go through Samaria. So he came to a town in Samaria called Sychar, near the plot of ground Jacob had given to his son Joseph. Jacob's well was there, and Jesus, tired as he was from the journey, sat down by the well. It was about the sixth hour. When a Samaritan woman came to draw water, Jesus said to her, "Will you give me a drink?" (His disciples had gone into the town to buy food.) The Samaritan woman said to him, "You are a Jew and I am a Samaritan woman. How can you ask me for a drink?" (For Jews do not associate with Samaritans.) Jesus answered her, "If you knew the gift of God and who it is that asks you for a drink, you would have asked him and he would have given you living water." "Sir," the woman said, "you have nothing to draw with and the well is deep. Where can you get this living water? Are you greater than our father Jacob, who gave us the well and drank from it himself, as did also his sons and his flocks and herds?" Jesus answered, "Everyone who drinks this water will be thirsty again, but whoever drinks the water I give him will never thirst. Indeed, the water I give him will become in him a spring of water welling up to eternal life." The woman said to him, "Sir, give me this water so that I won't get thirsty and have to keep coming here to draw water." He told her, "Go, call your husband and come back." "I have no husband," she replied. Jesus said to her, "You are right when you say you have no husband. The fact is, you have had five husbands, and the man you now have is not your husband. What you have just said is quite true." "Sir," the woman said, "I can see that you are a prophet. Our fathers worshiped on this mountain, but you Jews claim that the place where we must worship is in Jerusalem." Jesus declared, "Believe me,

> woman, a time is coming when you will worship the Father neither on this mountain nor in Jerusalem. You Samaritans worship what you do not know; we worship what we do know, for salvation is from the Jews. Yet a time is coming and has now come when the true worshipers will worship the Father in spirit and truth, for they are the kind of worshipers the Father seeks. God is spirit, and his worshipers must worship in spirit and in truth" (John 4:1-24).

In the scripture above, the topic of worship arose, and in verses 19–21, the woman asked Jesus a question involving the most appropriate place to worship God. Was it on this mountain as her forefathers taught, or in Jerusalem like the Jews claimed? Notice Jesus's answer in verses 23–24…

"A time is coming and has now come when the true worshipers will worship the Father in spirit and truth, for they are the kind of worshipers the Father seeks. God is spirit, and his worshipers must worship in spirit and in truth" (John 4:23-24).

Jesus was speaking of a truth still unavailable to those under the old covenant, but as the new covenant would be initiated upon His death and resurrection, praise and worship would take on a whole new dimension—the dimension of the Spirit! No longer would it be confined or limited to one place or another in the physical realm, but it would be offered in spirit, or in the spiritual dimension of the heavenly tabernacle not made with human hands (as we've discussed in previous chapters).

Notice I *didn't say* the physical realm is unimportant or unnecessary. In fact, it is incredibly important that people assemble at set times in set locations, for the purpose of offering praise and worship to God. Gathering together in physical places provides much-needed accountability, community, and edification one to another. That said, the point I'm making is that worship in spirit is not only *physical* in nature, but also *spiritual* as we move about in a heavenly tabernacle. In addition, worship in spirit involves being led by or carried along by the Holy Spirit. To understand this, let's highlight one very important aspect of the Holy Spirit's nature.

The Holy Spirit Described as Water

Repeatedly throughout scripture, the Holy Spirit is likened to water. This is certainly not to imply that the Holy Spirit *is* water. The scriptures clearly teach that He is a Person—the Third Person of the trinity. However, the fact that scripture likens the Holy Spirit to water simply illustrates, in terms we can understand, how the Spirit moves and flows.

Often even young believers perceive a certain flow of the Spirit in corporate worship services or times of prayer. One can, in a sense, feel the flow of the Spirit.

In the passage already cited above, Jesus offered the Samaritan woman living water that would well up inside, quench her spiritual thirst, and bring eternal life. Here, Jesus was speaking of the born-again experience, where the Holy Spirit comes to dwell within a believer at his or her point of conversion.

Later, Jesus was teaching the crowd gathered to celebrate the Feast of Tabernacles; notice what He said…

"On the last and greatest day of the Feast, Jesus stood and said in a loud voice, 'If anyone is thirsty, let him come to me and drink. Whoever believes in me, as the scripture has said, streams of living water will flow from within him.' By this he meant the Spirit, whom those who believed in him were later to receive." (John 7:37–39).

Jesus referred to *streams of living water* within us, and verse 39 specifically states that He was talking about the Spirit.

A simple word study on "spirit" reveals scores of further examples in both the Old and New Testaments. We find numerous references, comparing the Spirit with things such as water, streams, rivers, refreshing, and the like. This is an important thing to keep in mind as we consider what it means to worship in spirit and attempt to understand how we flow with the Spirit down particular pathways during praise and worship experiences.

There Is a River

In addition to the Holy Spirit being likened to rivers and streams, scripture clearly states that *there is a river* that flows from the throne of God in His temple. Read the scripture below...

> The man brought me back to the entrance of the temple, and I saw water coming out from under the threshold of the temple toward the east (for the temple faced east). The water was coming down from under the south side of the temple, south of the altar. He then brought me out through the north gate and led me around the outside to the outer gate facing east, and the water was flowing from the south side. As the man went eastward with a measuring line in his hand, he measured off a thousand cubits and then led me through water that was ankle-deep. He measured off another thousand cubits and led me through water that was knee-deep. He measured off another thousand and led me through water that was up to the waist. He measured off another thousand, but now it was a river that I could not cross, because the water had risen and was deep enough to swim in—a river that no one could cross. He asked me, "Son of man, do you see this?" Then he led me back to the bank of the river. When I arrived there, I saw a great number of trees on each side of the river. He said to me, "This water flows toward the eastern region and goes down into the Arabah, where it enters the Sea. When it empties into the Sea, the water there becomes fresh. Swarms of living creatures will live wherever the river flows. There will be large numbers of fish, because this water flows there and makes the salt water fresh; so where the river flows everything will live. Fishermen will stand along the shore; from En Gedi to En Eglaim there will be places for spreading

> nets. The fish will be of many kinds—like the fish of the Great Sea. But the swamps and marshes will not become fresh; they will be left for salt. Fruit trees of all kinds will grow on both banks of the river. Their leaves will not wither, nor will their fruit fail. Every month they will bear, because the water from the sanctuary flows to them. Their fruit will serve for food and their leaves for healing" (Ezekiel 47:1-12).

Notice that we are brought into an apocalyptic vision of the temple's entrance, where Ezekiel saw water streaming eastward from under the south side of the temple threshold (41:2). The stream passed by the south side of the altar of sacrifice, through the outer court, and out of the temple complex, along the south side of the eastern gate. A divine messenger instructed Ezekiel to explore the extent of this stream, and a measuring line was used to mark off four intervals (approximately one third of a mile each). At every interval, the messenger took Ezekiel into the stream to examine its depths, which were ever increasing. At the final interval, the stream had become a river of such magnitude that it could not be crossed.

The river continued to flow southeasterly toward the Arabah, the desolate Jordan Valley Rift that extends south to the Red Sea. Finally, the river flowed into the Dead Sea and caused that sea to live!

Many trees lined the river's sides, and every kind of fruit tree grew at its banks. The leaves of these trees never withered, and they actually provided healing. The fruit was perennial, bearing every month of the year, and it served as nourishing food for the inhabitants of the land. The entire Dead Sea was healed by the river, causing the water to teem with marine life, to the extent that fishermen fished from En Gedi to En Eglaim, catching a great variety of sea creatures (verses 9 and 10). Everywhere the river flowed, it took its life-giving power, except for the swamps and marshes, which were left for salt.

In light of Ezekiel's vision, consider the following about the river as applied to the pathway of praise and worship:

- The *source* of the life-giving water was the temple—the throne room—the very presence of God!
- There were differing *depths* to examine, which expanded out to the point that exploration would be inexhaustible.
- Ezekiel, by choice, had to *submit* to the leading of the messenger as he attempted to travel to ever-increasing depths.
- The river had a distinct *flow*, or current.
- The river produced life-giving *results* (fruitfulness, growth, provision, and healing), even having the power to make that which was dead come alive.
- The only place the river didn't bring life was in the swamps and marshes, where there was *stagnation* because of the absence of an outlet. (What flowed in didn't flow out.)

> Revelation 22:1–2, 12, 17: "Then the angel showed me the river of the water of life, as clear as crystal, flowing from the throne of God and of the Lamb down the middle of the great street of the city. On each side of the river stood the tree of life, bearing twelve crops of fruit, yielding its fruit every month. And the leaves of the tree are for the healing of the nations … 'Behold, I am coming soon!'… The Spirit and the bride say, 'Come!' And let him who hears say, 'Come!' Whoever is thirsty, let him come; and whoever wishes, let him take the free gift of the water of life."

References to the river also extend to the New Testament, where John the Revelator sees the river and writes about it. (Refer to Revelation 22:1–2, 12, 17.)

There is a river! And that river has to do with the Spirit of God, the presence of God, and our decision to enter in and yield to its flow of increasing, deepening dimensions!

Furthermore, the river provides life and healing, strength and joy, restoration and comfort, fruitfulness and power. Incredible!

The Never-Ending Pathway into His Presence

Why are we talking so much about the river of God? Well, I believe the pathway we travel as we praise and worship God is *none other than the river itself!*

We choose to enter in and are led by the Spirit of God to different depths—different shore-scapes—sometimes a soft, gentle flow—other times an ever-increasing torrent. The deeper we go, the less footing we have, and subsequently, the less we are able to depend upon our own strength or ability. The deeper we go, the more we must surrender. And God is *so* loving and patient, no matter what depth we choose—no matter how dead and barren our circumstances seem—if we're in the river, we will experience life and fruitfulness to one degree or another. The only exception seems to be when we've allowed ourselves to grow stagnant. In that instance, like the swamps and marshes of Ezekiel's vision, we may be exposed to the river, but the water becomes lifeless within us because there is no outlet to complete its flow through us.

Having said all of this, let me make the following important observations about worship in spirit.

Many believers who do not fully understand Spirit-led worship feel as if the flow is stopped by a leader in certain instances. For example, a praise and worship time seems to be flowing, and then all of a sudden, the worship leader says, "Now let's greet one another," or he or she directs the people to move into a different part of the service.

Two statements concerning this:

1. The flow of the river never ends. Praise and worship around His throne is eternal. So, anytime we choose to exit a season of praise and worship, we are breaking the flow to an extent.
2. Having said this, it is important to realize that the flow of the river *does* crescendo and decrescendo (increase and decrease in intensity). Thus, it is best to exit at a point when we sense the Holy Spirit releasing us to move on to other things—a point when He has completed the immediate thing He was doing. Keep in mind, this is *always* a judgment call, and there is a lot of room for human error. Be merciful to leadership, others in the congregation, and yourself as we together learn how to flow in the depths of the river of praise and worship!

Clearly, worship in spirit has a lot to do with being led by the Spirit—listening with sensitivity to His voice—which leads me to another point.

Flowing in Prophetic Worship

Bob Sorge says, "To move prophetically in worship is to move with an awareness of the desire and leading of the Holy Spirit … to discern the direction of the Spirit, and to lead God's people into a fuller participation of that."[12] All of this is made possible *by*, and enhanced *through*, the gifts of the Spirit found in 1 Corinthians 12:7–11, as they are used alongside musical praise and worship. See the scripture to the left.

> 1 Corinthians 12:7–11: "Now to each one the manifestation of the Spirit is given for the common good. To one there is given through the Spirit the message of wisdom, to another the message of knowledge by means of the same Spirit, to another faith by the same Spirit, to another gifts of healing by that one Spirit, to another miraculous powers, to another prophecy, to another distinguishing between spirits, to another speaking in different kinds of tongues, and to still another the interpretation of tongues. All these are the work of one and the same Spirit, and he gives them to each one, just as he determines."

Sorge goes on to say, "By playing [or singing] with sensitivity to the Spirit, a prophetic musician can 'unlock' a worship service," fostering an environment where the Spirit can move among His people.[13] As spiritual gifts are released, the congregation is inspired to connect more deeply with the Lord.

Numerous examples of musicians releasing prophetic worship are found in scripture. Among them, 1 Chronicles 25 tells of how David and the leadership of Israel set aside certain musical Levites specifically for the ministry of prophesying, accompanied by harps, lyres, and cymbals. Also, 1 Samuel 10 recounts Saul's anointing as king over Israel. As he (Saul) was approaching a Philistine outpost, he met a procession of prophets coming down from the high place with lyres, tambourines, flutes, and harps, and they were prophesying. As this prophetic flow was released, Saul, too, began to prophesy, and he was changed into a different person.

---

[12] Bob Sorge, *Exploring Worship: A Practical Guide to Praise & Worship* (Lee's Summit, MO: Oasis House, 2000), 125.

[13] Ibid., 129.

Now, let's turn to some practical application.

How can we begin to identify some of the pathways, or depths, that the Holy Spirit may be leading us into corporately, as a church body, during times of praise and worship?

The diagram below may provide some help.

The large box represents the presence of God, where we enter in through praise, worship, and prayer by the blood of Jesus. It is the true holy of holies in the true tabernacle of heaven.

Once we are there, we are "in the river." At that point, the Holy Spirit may direct us personally or corporately down one of many paths or tributaries.

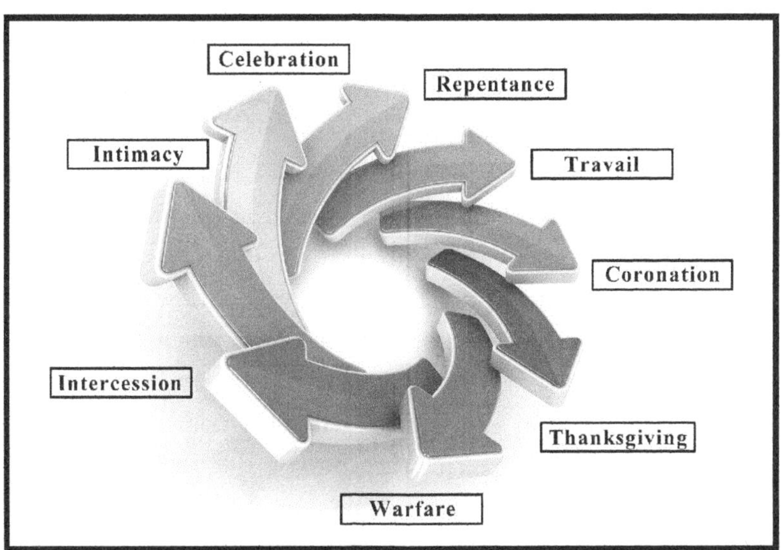

Numerous arrows unwinding from the center demonstrate multiple possibilities before us. In reality, these possibilities are innumerable. Each small box identifies one path that any given arrow may lead to.

What is *not* shown on the diagram is that each little box can actually become its own core, with innumerable arrows or paths spiraling out from its center. Thus, the combinations are endless. One path may flow into another, then another, and on and on until we step out of the river!

Think of it this way:

You've decided to step into the river of God's presence… First, you pass through His gates with thanksgiving and move into His courts with praise… Then, as you progress into more intimate worship, you eventually find yourself in the holy of holies, at the foot of His throne, where the river flows… You step in, and the Holy Spirit begins to move you to a place of deep humility and confession of personal sins… You foster the living interaction with God by offering yourself wholeheartedly as a living sacrifice… Moments pass… The river grows deeper and more powerful… Through the Holy Spirit, Jesus speaks a word of truth to you… He is birthing freedom in some area of your life… At that moment, the river crests, and you begin to head downstream… Water splashes across your face as you find yourself in joyous celebration and praise for the things God has just accomplished in your life… Time passes… The river slows… You find yourself in a pool of rest and peace… You enjoy this place for a season, breathing in the fresh air and taking in the beautiful scenery as you slowly drift close to shore and pass underneath the delicate branches of a weeping willow… The current sweeps you gently through them, and you notice the glistening beauty of the moist leaves as they brush across your face… Then, you hear a sound… You feel it in your spirit… You look out into the middle of the river… The Holy Spirit is urging you into deeper waters, out into the depths of intercession for a member of your family… Almost before you know it, you realize you are yards from shore… You look back at the willow, but with love and determination, you sense a call to war against the evils that are trying to destroy your loved one… After a couple seconds of hesitation, you yield to the flow… Deeper and deeper you go… Farther and farther you travel… Now, you are tempted to fear because your feet have not touched bottom for quite some time, and the current is growing stronger… Suddenly, you realize your head is *under water*… You are tempted to panic, but somehow you know you are safe… The Holy Spirit urges you to press in… You begin to pray passionately for your loved one… You cry out in travail… You thrash your arms and legs against the current to stay focused… Finally, your head comes to the surface, and you take a deep breath… You receive encouragement from the Holy Spirit, that your prayers are having an impact… You continue pressing in… under the water… out… under… back out… Finally, things become still… The river has slowed again… Something has happened… Something has changed as a result of your prayer… You don't even know entirely what's taken place, but something is different, and breakthrough has come… Your limbs ache somewhat, and your breathing has increased… But His presence is there… You have been sustained by His power… Slowly, you drift close to shore… Your feet begin to brush the sandy bottom… For now, you climb onto the bank, look downstream, and say softly to yourself, "I wonder what is just around the next bend?"… Then, turning toward the path that leads home, you begin to walk away from the river, thinking to yourself, "Maybe tomorrow will be the day I experience His river in all its glory and fullness. Maybe tomorrow will be the day I never have to get out of the river again!"

Summation

1. The kind of worshipers the Father seeks are those who worship Him in spirit and truth (John 4:1–24).
2. To worship in spirit is to understand the spiritual nature of our worship, and also to be led by or carried along by the Holy Spirit.
3. Throughout scripture, the Holy Spirit is likened to water, streams, rivers, and refreshing.
4. There *is* a river that flows from the throne of God; its existence is confirmed by the psalmists, several prophets, Jesus himself, and John the Revelator.
5. Praise and worship brings us into this river. Once there, the Holy Spirit may lead us down different pathways or tributaries, and to varying depths or strengths of current.
6. Though the flow of this river never ends, we must choose to exit at appropriate times.

7. Prophetic worship is made possible *by*, and enhanced *through*, the gifts of the Spirit; prophetic musicians create an environment for the Spirit to move among His people.
8. As we are sensitive to the Holy Spirit, the paths that He leads us down, individually or corporately, are innumerable; one path flows into another, then another, and so on.
9. Understanding more about how to enter the river and how to worship once we're there helps us approach praise and worship experiences with great anticipation, being led on fresh interactive journeys with the Lord!

Devotional Exercise

Begin to pay attention to some of the pathways you travel during a given time of praise and worship. Take note of various things you sense along the way: feelings, visions, etc. What is most enjoyable about the journey? What are some obstacles you encounter along the way? What are some lessons the Lord is attempting to teach you?

Study Guide Questions—Chapter 5

1. In your own words, what does it mean to worship God in spirit?
2. In what ways can you apply Ezekiel's vision of the river to your praise and worship experiences?
3. During personal and corporate praise and worship times, how can you cultivate greater sensitivity to the Holy Spirit?
4. Thinking back to your own experiences, what are some of the pathways the Holy Spirit has led you down (listed on page 65)?
    a) List all the pathways you've traveled.
    b) Describe one in as much detail as you can.
5. Spend some time thinking about other possible pathways (apart from those listed on page 65), and write them down.
6. Of all the possible pathways listed in questions 4 and 5 above, which is your favorite and *why* (whether you have experienced this pathway or not)?

7. Of all the possible pathways listed in questions 4 and 5 above, which is the hardest for you and *why* (whether you have experienced this pathway or not)?
8. How will your life be different as a result of this chapter?

SET LIST EXERCISES

Directions:

1. For each set list provided, describe the interaction taking place between God and the worshiper.
2. Chart the progression, from the outer court, through the holy place, and into the holy of holies.
3. List biblical references and/or scriptural principles found in each song.

(Use a separate sheet of paper if necessary.)

Worship service
February 22, 2015

"God's Great Dance Floor"
"Wake"
"10,000 Reasons"
"Breathe"
"Your Great Name"

"God's Great Dance Floor"
I'm coming back to the start
Where You found me
I'm coming back to Your heart
Now I surrender
Take me, this is all I can bring
You'll never stop loving us no matter how far we run
You'll never give up on us, all of heaven shouts, let the future begin
I feel alive, I come alive, I am alive on God's great dance floor

Copyright 2013 Gloworks, S.D.G. Publishing, sixsteps music, Thankyou Music, and worshiptogether.com songs

"Wake"

At break of day, in hope we rise
We speak Your name, we lift our eyes
Tune our hearts into Your beat
Where we walk there You'll be
With fire in our eyes our lives alight
Your love untamed, it's blazing out
The streets will glow forever bright
Your glory's breaking through the night
You will never fade away, Your love is here to stay
By my side, in my life, shining through me ev'ry day
You wake within me, wake within me
You're in my heart forever
Forever, forever, forever in Your love

Copyright 2013 Hillsong Music Publishing

"10,000 Reasons"

The sun comes up, it's a new day dawning
It's time to sing Your song again
Whatever may pass and whatever lies before me
Let me be singing when the evening comes
Bless the Lord, oh my soul, oh my soul
Worship His holy name
Sing like never before, oh my soul
I'll worship Your holy name

Copyright 2011 Atlas Mountain Songs, Said And Done Music, sixsteps music, Thankyou Music, and worshiptogether.com songs

"Breathe"

This is the air I breathe, this is the air I breathe
Your holy presence living in me
This is my daily bread, this is my daily bread
Your very Word spoken to me
And I, I'm desperate for You
And I, I'm lost without You

Copyright 1995 Vineyard Music USA

"Your Great Name"
Lost are saved, find their strength at the sound of Your great name
All condemned feel no shame at the sound of Your great name
Ev'ry fear has no place at the sound of Your great name
The enemy, he has to leave at the sound of Your great name
Jesus, worthy is the Lamb that was slain for us
The Son of God and man
You are high and lifted up
And all the world will praise Your great name
Redeemer, my Healer
Lord Almighty
Defender, my Savior, You are my King

Copyright 2008 Integrity's Praise! Music and TwoNords Music

Worship service
November 11, 2007

"Follow the Son"
"My Savior Lives"
"How Great Is Our God"
"At the Cross"
"Here I Am to Worship"

"Follow the Son"
You are the Light that guides my way through fear
I know my path will lead me to the King
And all the world will bow to worship You
You are the God that changed the world through one Holy Son
You gave ev'rything so all the world will bow in awe of You
You came down through grace to show a better way
I'll follow the Son, He's the only One, let His kingdom come
I'm giving it all to the One I love
I'll follow the Son, Jesus, Holy One, let Your will be done
I give it all to You
You are ev'rything to me, hey, hey, You are ev'rything to me, hey, hey
You are ev'rything to me, hey, hey, You are ev'rything to me

Copyright 2005 Hillsong Music Publishing

"My Savior Lives"

Our God will reign forever, and all the world will know His name
Ev'ryone together sing the song of the redeemed
I know that my Redeemer lives
And now I stand on what He did
My Savior, my Savior lives
Ev'ry day a brand new chance to say
"Jesus, You are the Only Way!"
My Savior, my Savior lives
My Savior lives, my Savior lives, my Savior lives

Copyright 2006 Integrity Music Publishing

"How Great Is Our God"

The splendor of the King clothed in majesty
Let all the earth rejoice, all the earth rejoice
He wraps Himself in light, and darkness tries to hide
It trembles at His voice, trembles at His voice
How great is our God, sing with me
How great is our God, and all will see
How great, how great is our God
Name above all names, worthy of all praise
My heart will sing, "How great is our God!"

Copyright 2004 sixsteps music, worshiptogether.com songs, and Wondrously Made Songs

"At the Cross"

Oh Lord, You've searched me, You know my way
Even when I fail You, I know You love me
At the cross I bow my knee where Your blood was shed for me
There's no greater love than this
You have overcome the grave, Your glory fills the highest place
What can separate me now
You tore the veil, You made a way
When You said that it is done

Copyright 2006 Hillsong Music Publishing and Wondrous Worship

"Here I Am to Worship"
Light of the world, You stepped down into darkness
Opened my eyes, let me see
Beauty that made this heart adore You
Hope of a life spent with You
Here I am to worship, here I am to bow down
Here I am to say that You're my God
You're altogether lovely, altogether worthy
Altogether wonderful to me
I'll never know how much it cost
To see my sin upon that cross

Copyright 2000 Thankyou Music

Chapter 6

THE PRACTICE OF PRAISE: WORSHIPING IN TRUTH

Part 1

> John 3:5–8: "Jesus answered, 'I tell you the truth, no one can enter the kingdom of God unless he is born of water and the Spirit. Flesh gives birth to flesh, but the Spirit gives birth to spirit. You should not be surprised at my saying, "You must be born again." The wind blows wherever it pleases. You hear its sound, but you cannot tell where it comes from or where it is going. So it is with everyone born of the Spirit.'"
>
> 1 Corinthians 2:14: "The man without the Spirit does not accept the things that come from the Spirit of God, for they are foolishness to him, and he cannot understand them, because they are spiritually discerned."

In chapter 5, we covered the topic of worshiping in spirit. The lesson provided some explanation about the first half of John 4:23–24, which indicates the kind of worshipers the Father seeks: those who "worship in spirit."

1. We learned that we must be born of the Spirit, or born again, to worship in spirit. (See John 3:5–8, 1 Corinthians 1:14.)
2. Also, we learned that there is a river that flows from the throne of God. As we come into God's presence through praise and worship, we can enter that river and be moved along to varying degrees of depth and purpose. The Holy Spirit may lead us to places of intercession, celebration, confession, or one of several other "tributaries" according to the plan of God at that particular moment. We just need to

choose to enter the river and get into the flow. This happens as we submit to the direction of the Holy Spirit. Corporately, such direction comes through the pastor, worship leader, or individuals operating in the gifts of the Spirit.

The Practice of Praise

This chapter focuses not on the *pathway* (the river and yielding to it) but primarily on the *practice* of praise (*how* we are to praise and worship and *what we are to do* as we are being led along in the river).

The second half of John 4:24 indicates that the Father is not only looking for those who will worship Him in *spirit*, but also those who will worship Him in *truth*.

Here's a working definition of worship in truth, which provides a foundation for our discussion:

To worship God in truth means we are motivated by biblical truth as we worship Jesus, the Living Truth. We freely express our devotion through biblical parameters while exercising integrity of heart, mind, and speech.

In the next three chapters, I want to fully unpack this definition, but first let me explain how worshiping in truth actually safeguards against certain extremes.

As we said in the beginning, praise and worship often exemplifies one of two extremes: the "experimental, emotional approach," where individuals throw all caution to the wind, or the "ultraconservative approach," where there is a need to control the situation.

The Experimental, Emotional Approach

In this approach, emotional expression is seen as the prime directive. Decency and order are thrown out the window, and individuals simply do everything under the sun. How one is "led" becomes the standard of truth!

Please understand that wholeheartedly worshiping in spirit *does* put us in a place of minimal control as we abandon ourselves to the depths of the river. And, in such a position, we are very vulnerable to emotionalism and weirdness! But this is exactly why we must have guidance of the truth along with freedom of the Spirit.

The Ultraconservative Approach

Taking this approach really defies the whole idea of sacrificial praise, crucifying our pride, moving beyond shallow, rational waters and actually "offending the box" (i.e., our comfort zone). Remember, true worship *always* requires a sacrifice, and public expression demands the humbling of our pride.

For those who choose to adopt such an approach, emotional expression is seen as "carnal" (unspiritual). Paul's exhortation to let everything be done is dismissed because we draw our own conclusions about what is decent and in order. The real danger of this is the limitation we place upon the moving of the Spirit.

The truth is, God cannot be placed in a convenient box where we keep control of His every move! He will do things that stretch our faith and take us beyond what we are used to!

At one point or another, most worship leaders have been tempted to control a situation with the right song or right exhortation instead of allowing the Holy Spirit to work in the hearts of His people. It's difficult to relinquish control at times. But fostering a polished, controlled praise and worship experience can actually be destructive because leaders *think* they are making a spiritual impact when, in reality, they are giving people a man-made production.

What if the Holy Spirit impresses a worship leader to have everyone in the congregation spin around in a circle two times? Too weird? Well, before you say yes, consider how Naaman felt in 2 Kings 5, when he came to Elisha to be healed of leprosy, and Elisha told him to dip into the Jordan River seven times. This was *not* what Naaman had in mind. It was not rational for someone with open sores to dip into the Jordan River, which was anything but sanitary. How silly these instructions must have sounded!

Likewise, consider the account of Gideon in Judges chapter 7. He started with an army of thirty-two thousand men, and God told him there were too many to fight the battle! And after twenty-two thousand left, God instructed him to watch how the men lapped water, in order to further diminish the group! Then, after Gideon's army was successfully whittled down to a mere three hundred men, God announced some pretty ridiculous battle plans; He actually expected Gideon to buy into the idea that three hundred men would defeat an entire Midianite army with trumpets and jars containing torches!

A miracle in its own right, Gideon believed God (though his faith was severely tested, and the Lord had to provide signs that this was, in fact, His will). In the end, Gideon obeyed, and the Lord did exactly what He said He would do.

The point is not how many men fought or which weapons were used; God could have defeated the Midianites with a single soldier wielding a blanket. And in Naaman's case, there was nothing special about the Jordan River; God could have easily healed Naaman with the dew of the morning. The point *was* and *still is* obedience. Will we simply obey, no matter how irrational the promptings seem?

If you want to know why there is such *little power* in the church today, I am convinced it has to do with *little obedience*. In our culture, people resist being told what to do by anyone, even church leadership. Pastoral requests and messages given through gifts of the Spirit are treated with indifference. The truth is, if the Spirit is prompting a leader to have us stand on our heads as an act of worship, the only decent and orderly thing to do is just that! The most reverent thing we could *ever* do is obey! (I'm, of course, providing an extreme example, but it nonetheless proves the point. And remember the unconventional things the Lord asked Naaman and Gideon to do.)

Some may object and say, "It's not good to draw attention to yourself." True, but my experience has often been that the biggest reason people draw attention to themselves in a time of praise and worship is due to the following: when the Spirit prompts, 90 percent disobey, while the 10 percent (or less) who *do* obey are rebuked for drawing attention to themselves!

Again, almost without exception, anytime the Spirit moves in a powerful way (seen throughout scripture and in every major revival of church history), the direction or prompting that ends up being a powerful catalyst is typically very unconventional!

Can you imagine Pastor Joshua instructing his congregation that it was God's plan for them to march around the wall of a city for seven days without saying a thing—then, the seventh trip around on the seventh day, they were to look at the wall and yell at it, expecting it to fall? Yeah, right! If Joshua would have been leading the typical congregation today, people would have brazenly told him he was out of his mind. They would have rebelled less than ten minutes into the first trip around the wall, on the very first day. Silence would have been broken by people's complaints about how dumb this was. Some might have sat down rebelliously, folding their arms and shaking their heads in disapproval of the foolish instructions the pastor was giving them!

Yes, the examples I've provided are all found in the Old Testament, but these scenarios are no more ridiculous than Jesus spitting in the dirt and rubbing mud on a blind man's eyes, or Jesus telling Peter to go down to the lake and find a coin in the mouth of a fish. Jesus could have just as easily told Peter to sit down under the fifth olive tree he came to, and a bird would land on his shoulder, chirp three times, and spit a coin out of its mouth. The packaging did not matter. What mattered was Peter's willingness to obey.

It's obedience! It's faith! That's what God responds to!

Yes, order is important. But let it be organization without suffocation! Maturity in worship, worshiping in spirit and truth, requires not digging your heels into the ultraconservative extreme!

So how does biblical praise and worship differ?

1. Our praise and worship must be motivated by biblical truth.

If we are going to take seriously Jesus's words to the woman at the well in John 4:23–24, that the Father seeks worshipers who will worship Him in spirit *and in truth,* we must ask ourselves the question, "What is truth?"

Jesus identifies "truth" very clearly in a later part of John, in His prayer to the Father for all believers…

"Sanctify them by the truth; your word is truth" (John 17:17).

Simply put, the Father is seeking worshipers who will worship in spirit and according to the truth contained in His Word!

Listen, our motivation must not be emotion but, rather, a deep understanding of and personal adherence to the truth of God's Word. Authentic praise and worship will be emotional, but the emotion will be a natural by-product of the truth that comes alive to us as we worship.

Before a hand is ever raised… before an instrument is played… before a shout… praise and worship begins internally as our hearts grab a hold of (1) some aspect of biblical truth such as salvation, God's promise to provide, the Lord's keeping power or (2) some aspect of His character such as His faithfulness, His mercy, or His love. Then the truth produces emotion, which should, in turn, be expressed.

Listen to what A. W. Tozer says about the negative result of not worshiping according to the truth of who God is and what He does:

> "We can't worship these days because we do not have a high enough opinion of God. He has been reduced, modified, edited, changed and amended until He is not the God Isaiah saw high and lifted up but something else … Worship rises and falls in the church altogether depending on whether the idea of God is low or high."[14]

We must have the right idea of God when we worship—the truth of who He is and what He does. This is clearly portrayed in His Word.

Here's another way of looking at it. John 1:1 tells us that Jesus Himself is the Word who was with God the Father in the very beginning. If the Word is truth, then shouldn't Jesus be at the center of our praise and worship? If He isn't occupying a central focus, are we really worshiping in truth?

---

[14] A. W. Tozer, "Worship: The Chief End of Man," *Sermon #5* (Toronto, Canada: Avenue Road Church, 1962).

Let's look at a song example ...

"He Set Me Free"
Once like a bird in prison I dwelt
No freedom from my sorrow I felt
But Jesus came and listened to me
Glory to God, He set me free

He set me free, yes, He set me free
He broke the bonds of prison for me
I'm glory-bound, my Jesus to see
Glory to God, He set me free

Copyright 1967 Bridge Building Music (adm. by Brentwood-Benson Music Publishing)

In "He Set Me Free," we discover the truth of God's Word—that Jesus has:

- Come to bring release to the prisoners (Luke 4:18)
- Set us free from the law of sin and death (Romans 8:2)
- Given indisputable evidence of our freedom (John 8:36)

> Luke 4:18: "The Spirit of the Lord is on me, because he has anointed me to preach good news to the poor. He has sent me to proclaim freedom for the prisoners and recovery of sight for the blind, to release the oppressed."
>
> Romans 8:2: "Because through Christ Jesus the law of the Spirit of life set me free from the law of sin and death."
>
> John 8:36: "If the Son sets you free, you will be free indeed."

That should *definitely* motivate us to offer an emotional response. (If it doesn't, then something's wrong!)

(You may or may not know "He Set Me Free." It's an oldie. Still, you could come to the same conclusions about newer praise and worship songs, such as "I Am Free" or "Alive.")

You can sing it country, rock 'n' roll, opera, rap, fast, slow, loud, soft, guitar-driven, or piano-driven. You can know it by heart or read it for the first time on the screen Sunday morning. The point is, *truth* should produce emotion. Style and delivery are subservient to the Word of God.

When I say "style" and "delivery," I'm referring to negotiable methods that will change from one context to another. These not only include musical elements such as genre, tempo, volume, and instrumentation, but also elements such as service order, leadership style, level of formality, use of technology, and incorporation of nonmusical arts. We tend to major on the minors, but scripture does not major on any of these things.

What's important is that the worshiper is responding to the nonnegotiable Word found in our praise and worship songs. And this emotional response is nothing more than simple obedience—*most of the time.* But let's explore further.

At some point, you will have to give a response that seems contrary to your circumstances and feelings. I call this "faith praise," and it extends beyond simple obedience because what you are proclaiming and what the situation actually looks like are two entirely different things.

Faith praise looks like this: When you're sick, you sing, "I believe You're my Healer." When it seems God has let you down, you sing, "Great is thy faithfulness." When you're feeling weak, you sing, "You are my shield, my strength, my portion, deliverer," and worship according to the *truth* of God's Word, which declares…

"That is why, for Christ's sake, I delight in weaknesses, in insults, in hardships, in persecutions, in difficulties. For when I am weak, then I am strong" (2 Corinthians 12:10).

Worshiping in truth means we are motivated by biblical truth, which produces emotion, but then:

2. We must express this emotion freely within biblical parameters.

A mature response to truth will almost always lead to emotion, and this is where physical expression comes into play. It's the external part of our praise and worship.

Biblical Worship Includes Vocal and Physical Expression

Praise and worship is not confined to silent adoration or mental ascent. Twice in his letters to the early church, Paul instructs people to speak to one another with psalms, hymns, and spiritual songs, which foster Spirit-filled living in the community of believers. Hebrews 13:15 declares that a sacrifice of praise is "the fruit of our lips."

Taken a step further, we are instructed (commanded) to *sing* to God over fifty times in scripture. And this singing is not just a subjective point of preference (reserved for those who can do it well), but it's a natural and appropriate expression of our love for God.

Furthermore, praise and worship isn't limited to vocal expression, but it should involve the entire body!

See Romans 6:11–13, 19 to the right.

> Romans 6:11–13: "In the same way, count yourselves dead to sin but alive to God in Christ Jesus. Therefore do not let sin reign in your mortal body so that you obey its evil desires. Do not offer the parts of your body to sin, as instruments of wickedness, but rather offer yourselves to God, as those who have been brought from death to life; and offer the parts of your body to him as instruments of righteousness."
>
> Romans 6:19: "I put this in human terms because you are weak in your natural selves. Just as you used to offer the parts of your body in slavery to impurity and to ever-increasing wickedness, so now offer them in slavery to righteousness leading to holiness."

Expressions of Praise and Worship

When a worshiper conducts himself or herself in ways that are appropriate during times of praise and worship, several beautiful expressions may result. God's Word instructs us to clap or lift our hands; shout; kneel; bow or raise our heads; dance; leap; lie prostrate; play musical instruments; sing psalms, hymns, and spiritual songs; speak forth His greatness, and so on.

Keeping this in mind, let's consider what was said earlier in this lesson. It is not out-of-the-question for the Holy Spirit to prompt us to express ourselves in an *unusual* manner. However, He will never prompt us to express ourselves in a manner that violates the Word. Praise and worship is an engagement with God on terms that He sets forth in His instruction manual, the Bible.

So what parameters does the Bible establish? Well, there are many different Hebrew and Greek words, all translated "praise," in our English Bibles. One word, though, denotes praising God in a completely different way than another word. For example, in one instance, we read that we should "praise" the Lord, and the Hebrew word *shabach* is being used, which means to shout praises. In another instance, we are instructed to "praise" the Lord, and the Hebrew word *barak* is being used, which means to humbly bow in honor and congratulations. These and other words will be explored in later chapters.

For now, simply understand that biblical expressions of praise and worship abound, and all of them are pleasing to God and serve as His prescribed methods of appropriate expression. Thus, we shouldn't treat them as items on a menu, from which we pick and choose based on personal taste and preference.

We don't treat any other body of scripture with a "menu approach." We are all supposed to be holy, to pray, to love the Lord with all our heart, to offer up our bodies as living sacrifices. We are all supposed to be witnesses, to bear one another's burdens and forgive each other. Husbands are supposed to love their wives; wives must love their husbands, etc.

Colossians 3:5–8: "Put to death, therefore, whatever belongs to your earthly nature: sexual immorality, impurity, lust, evil desires and greed, which is idolatry. Because of these, the wrath of God is coming. You used to walk in these ways, in the life you once lived. But now you must rid yourselves of all such things as these: anger, rage, malice, slander, and filthy language from your lips."

Consider Colossians 3:5–8 to the left, and ask yourself what would happen if Christians approached this list as a menu, from which they'd pick and choose things they were most comfortable doing—or they'd assume the things which didn't line up with their particular personality could be ignored.

Friend, scripture *commands* the following:

"*Clap* your hands, all you nations … *Shout* to God with cries of joy" (Psalm 47:1, emphasis added).

"*Speak* to one another with psalms, hymns and spiritual songs. *Sing* and *make music* in your heart to the Lord" (Ephesians 5:19, emphasis added).

"Let everything that has breath praise the Lord" (Psalm 150:6, emphasis added).

Let me be blatantly honest. "Worship however you want" has replaced corporate expressions of singing, shouting, clapping, dancing, kneeling, lifting hands, etc., and this has a lot to do with how leaders are stewarding times of praise and worship from the platform. It is my conviction that several of today's worship leaders are causing brothers and sisters to stumble because they are making non-offensive, "edifying" statements that encourage people to do whatever they want and call it worship, instead of requiring the biblical standard of worship to be upheld. As a result, there is a form of godliness without any power, and false worship that leads people astray.

Hearts are deceptive, and people are often very aware of their wants but very blind to their true needs. Let's not give people options that simply appeal to their fleshly wants; rather, let's line everything up with the patterns we find in the Word because those patterns are what please the Lord when it comes to corporate praise and worship.

If I love to do basket weaving, and I come together with other people who love to do basket weaving, it doesn't mean this activity is appropriate for corporate praise and worship. We can all feel encouraged and edified after our basket weaving sessions, but this "anything goes" approach can make our praise and worship times look very different from what God intends.

Of course, all of this leaves room for personal growth.

Everyone is at a different level of ability and freedom in expressing himself or herself in ways that are biblical. I'm not trying to heap condemnation on new believers or those who are just beginning to discover how they should express themselves during times of praise and worship, but if we are sincere in our desire to express ourselves *biblically*, we must be concerned with continual growth and increasing conformity to biblical patterns. The goal is true freedom in praise and worship. This is lived out as we come to the level of maturity where we're willing and able to follow each and every prompting of the Holy Spirit.

If a pastor, worship leader, or individual flowing in spiritual gifts encourages you to respond in a certain way, and the response is entirely biblical, the best thing you can do is obey. In a corporate setting, individuality needs to give way to a corporate flow, and this doesn't mean we're all doing the same thing, but it *does* mean we're heading in the same direction. The Holy Spirit will not prompt you to do something in opposition to what He is prompting the Body as a whole to do. In such instances, someone is missing it.

Let's continue to grow in grace and never lose sight of the fact that God is always more interested in our *direction* than He is in our *perfection*!

Maturity in worship is freedom to obey!

Summation

1. Worshiping God in truth means we are motivated by the truth of God's Word, as we worship Jesus, the Living Truth, while freely expressing our devotion within biblical parameters of behavior.
2. Worshiping in truth safeguards against the experimental, emotional extreme (where feelings become our prime directive) and also the ultraconservative extreme (where we are so reserved that we stifle the Spirit's work).
3. Obedience to the Holy Spirit is more critical to biblical praise and worship than the methods by which we express that obedience.
4. True praise and worship may be an expression of faith in response to the truth of God's Word, which is a step beyond simple obedience.
5. True praise and worship usually involves vocal and physical expression.
6. Biblical expressions of praise and worship should not be treated as items on a menu, from which we pick and choose to suit our personal tastes, but in a corporate setting, they become the parameters within which the worship leader facilitates Spirit-led praise and worship.

Devotional Exercises

1. Continue to notice which pathways you travel during a given time of praise and worship. Take note of various things you sense along the way: feelings, visions, etc. Answer these questions:
   - What is most enjoyable about your journey?
   - What are some obstacles you encounter along the way?
   - What are some lessons the Lord is attempting to teach you?

2. Make a list of things you could do—steps you could take—to grow in your praise and worship expression.

Study Guide Questions—Chapter 6

1. In your opinion, what are some of the dangers in adopting the experimental, emotional approach to praise and worship?
2. In your opinion, what are some of the dangers in adopting the ultraconservative approach to praise and worship?
3. How does a well-balanced biblical approach guard against these two extremes?
4. What is "faith praise"?
5. When it comes to vocal and physical expression (singing, clapping, lifting hands, shouting, bowing, etc.):
   a) Which expressions are easy for you at this stage of your growth?
   b) Which expression is the Holy Spirit currently prompting you to pursue?
6. What is meant by the statement "God is more interested in our *direction* than He is in our *perfection*"?

Chapter 7

THE PRACTICE OF PRAISE: WORSHIPING IN TRUTH

Part 2

In chapter 6, we covered the first aspect of worshiping in truth. Remember our foundational scripture…

"God is spirit, and his worshipers must worship in spirit *and in truth*" (John 4:24, emphasis added).

First, we learned that worshiping the Lord in truth means we are motivated by the truth, which is the Word of God, as we worship Jesus, the Living Truth.

Also, we learned that worshiping the Lord in truth involves biblical expression. We should read and study the Word of God to find out which physical expressions please the Lord—expressions that have been used by God's people throughout the ages. Generally speaking, our praise and worship will involve some physical response, and, very often, it will be highly emotional, though not emotion-driven. Remember, emotions are not bad or wrong when used in the right way.

Similarly, we learned that throughout scripture and major revivals in history, the Holy Spirit often orchestrated things that seemed foolish and tested a person's willingness to *simply obey*.

Finally, we learned that the role of leadership in any corporate praise and worship setting is to lead a congregation down specific pathways and, at times, encourage a specific response from the congregation as a whole. Unity and cooperation on the part of the congregation are extremely important during these times. The pastor or worship leader must always lead within the parameters of God's Word. And though he or she may ask the congregation to respond in a manner that seems abnormal or strange, the congregation must be willing to follow, with the understanding that the Holy Spirit will often use unconventional means and methods to test peoples' obedience. The pastor or worship leader will most often request a response that is specifically found in scripture (i.e., clapping, shouting, kneeling, dancing, etc.) and must *never* ask the people to violate the Word of God, though, at times, we may be asked to violate our comfort zones.

Here in chapter 7, we will further explore the issue of worshiping in truth, and, specifically, how we can worship with *integrity*... of heart... mind... and speech.

1. Worshiping with true integrity of *heart*

Worshiping in truth is, first and foremost, an issue of the heart. A wise man once said, "I don't care how high you jump, as long as you walk straight once you come down." Amidst raised hands and shouting, God is looking at each worshiper's heart! He is more concerned with what's happening on the inside than He is with outward appearance. This is clearly demonstrated in how David was chosen to be king over Israel. Outwardly, his brothers looked the part, but the Lord was attracted to David's heart—his true devotion. Listen to the heart cry of King David...

"Create in me a pure heart, O God, and renew a steadfast spirit within me. Do not cast me from your presence or take your Holy Spirit from me" (Psalm 51:10–11).

"Who may ascend the hill of the Lord? Who may stand in his holy place? He who has *clean hands* and a *pure heart*, who does not lift up his soul to an idol or swear by what is false" (Psalm 24:3–4, emphasis added).

In the same way, during His famous "Sermon on the Mount," Jesus said for all to hear…

"Blessed are the *pure in heart*, for they will *see God*" (Matthew 5:8, emphasis added).

Is this not the goal of every true worshiper—to rub shoulders with His Majesty?—to catch a glimpse of His glory?—to come into a living interaction?

Mark 7:18–23: "'Are you so dull?' he asked. 'Don't you see that nothing that enters a man from the outside can make him "unclean"? For it doesn't go into his heart but into his stomach, and then out of his body.' (In saying this, Jesus declared all foods "clean.") He went on: 'What comes out of a man is what makes him "unclean." For from within, out of men's hearts, come evil thoughts, sexual immorality, theft, murder, adultery, greed, malice, deceit, lewdness, envy, slander, arrogance and folly. All these evils come from inside and make a man "unclean."'"

Read Jesus's words about the importance of the heart, recorded in Mark 7:18–23 and to the left.

Now, ask yourself this question: what good is external worship if the heart is not pure?

Also see the words of the psalmist below, where we are taught how impurities in the heart actually destroy our ability to engage in a living interaction with God…

"Come and listen, all you who fear God; let me tell you what he has done for me. I cried out to him with my mouth; his praise was on my tongue. If I had cherished [harbored, held to] sin in my heart, the Lord would not have listened" (Psalm 66:16–18).

Clearly, worshiping with true integrity requires a *pure heart.*

And it also requires an *undivided heart…*

"Teach me your way, O LORD, and I will walk in your truth; give me an undivided heart, that I may fear your name. I will praise you, O Lord my God, with all my heart; I will glorify your name forever" (Psalm 86:11–12).

We can't serve two masters. We can't have one foot in the church and the other foot in the world. We can't have our hearts set on the Lord one day and want nothing to do with worship the next day. As David hungered for the presence of God, so we must pursue Him with passion and persistence, not becoming sidetracked for any reason.

2. Worshiping with true integrity of *mind*

Read Matthew 15:8–9 and Isaiah 29:13 to the right.

> Matthew 15:8–9: "These people honor me with their lips, but their hearts are far from me. They worship me in vain; their teachings are but rules taught by men."
>
> Isaiah 29:13: "The Lord says: 'These people come near to me with their mouth and honor me with their lips, but their hearts are far from me. Their worship of me is made up only of rules taught by men.'"

In Matthew 15, Jesus is speaking to the Pharisees and teachers. And in Isaiah 29, the prophet is rebuking the people of God. In both cases, the word "heart" indicates more than just the heart. It encompasses the whole idea of *mind, will, and emotions.* In other words, the people were worshiping with their mouths (externally), but they were not really tuned in. Internally, they were far from God. They weren't feeling any emotion for Him, had no desire to draw near to Him, and didn't even have their minds focused on what they were doing.

Concerning this latter point, have you ever been talking to someone and realized they weren't really listening to what you were saying because they were thinking, not about *your* words, but about what they were going to say as soon as you finished? Talking with someone who is preoccupied is a very frustrating experience! They still may nod or even speak, but you know they aren't really paying attention!

We must be careful not to do this to God during times of praise and worship. Remember, we're trying to engage in a living interaction!

- Do we worship God with our "lips," singing: "The enemy has been defeated" while thinking of how powerless we are in our current circumstances?
- Do we worship God with our "lips," singing: "Come bless the Lord, draw near to worship Christ the Lord" while thinking of lunch?
- Do we worship God with our "lips," singing: "Jesus is the sweetest name I know," then get mad at our kids and swear?

- Do we worship God with our "lips," singing: "All I need is you" while thinking, *If I could just have a new car… a job… kids that will listen*?

The question is, "Are we *thinking in our minds* what we are *saying with our lips*?" This is worshiping God with true integrity of mind.

3. Worshiping with true integrity of *speech*

Someone once said, "We do the most lying when we sing our songs." Think about how true that statement can be! In songs we hear every day, people promise this and promise that. In many *praise and worship* songs, we vow to surrender all to the Lord, to express our love in lavish ways, but do we always keep our promises?

Let's see what James has to say about the value of our speech…

"Above all, my brothers, do not swear—not by heaven or by earth or by anything else. *Let your 'Yes' be yes and your 'No', no*" (James 5:12, emphasis added).

Here, James is echoing the words of Jesus in Matthew 5:34–37, which forbid swearing (or the taking of oaths) altogether. Clearly, what is referred to in James and Matthew is the use of light, casual oaths in informal conversation—not formal oaths in such places as courts of law. (God himself is said to have taken a formal oath in Psalm 110:4.) The point is, rather than employing an oath to convince people that a statement is true, *the Christian should let his "yes" be yes—and his "no," no.* In other words, he should be honest in all his speech so that when he acknowledges something, people know it is unquestionably true.

In times past, a person's word was as good as gold. His or her word, along with a handshake, was sufficient to know that the individual would follow through on a particular promise. (Unfortunately, some of us only know "those days" from watching classic TV shows such as *The Waltons* or *Little House on the Prairie.*) The individual would go to great lengths to uphold his or her word, to protect his or her character or reputation. Not so today! The importance of personal integrity has diminished so drastically that we find ourselves needing formal contracts, drawn up by skilled legal consultants, to be sure there are no loopholes in a particular agreement, and even then, we're never entirely sure! As Christians living in this day and age, let's never forget that legal contracts may be required in certain situations, but we don't rely on them to hold us to our word; *rather, the word itself should govern our behavior.*

The truth is God puts high importance on words…

- In Genesis 1, God created the heavens and the earth by *speaking* them into being.
- In Matthew 8:8, the centurion said to Jesus, "Lord, I do not deserve to have you come under my roof. But just *say the word*, and my servant will be healed" (emphasis added).
- In Romans 10:9, Paul declared that "If you *confess with your mouth*, 'Jesus is Lord,' and believe in your heart that God raised Him from the dead, you will be saved." (emphasis added).

It's bad enough when those in *society* allow the integrity of their words to diminish in value and lose importance, but it's a sad day when *Christians* allow the cheapening of words to creep into their day-to-day lives.

Have you ever quickly made promises to people before you've prayerfully and carefully considered whether or not you could fulfill them? Have you told someone, "I'll be there," then called to say you would be late or not able to make it after all? I constantly wrestle with this in my own life, when I tell my wife I'll be home at five thirty, but instead I walk in the door at five forty-five. Or, I put one of my daughters to bed, and a few minutes later I hear, "Daddy," and I say something like, "I'll be there in a minute," knowing I plan to put her off until she falls asleep. Have you ever told an employer, friend, or family member that you would take care of something, then failed to follow through?

I think we all have!

Now, let's put all of this in the context of our praise and worship.

If we really believe praise and worship is an interaction with the Living God, can we, with integrity, really sing "I lift up my hands" and not lift our hands? Should we sing "I stand in awe of you" while we sit? Or, what if we sing "I'm falling on my knees"? Shouldn't our posture exemplify our words? What should we *do* as we sing "Clap your hands, all ye people… shout unto God with a voice of triumph… clap your hands, all ye people… shout unto God with a voice of praise"?

I'm not suggesting that we resort to a choreographed exercise, making everyone lift their hands at a particular moment or fall to their knees the instant they sing about that. As I've already stated, God is more concerned with what is going on in the heart than anything we *do* outwardly. However, I think it's safe to say that if we sing something and are *unwilling* to posture ourselves in a way that exemplifies what we are singing, this is a problem. The point is, we don't have to be paranoid about lifting our hands every time we sing that phrase, but if we *refuse* to lift our hands, there is a heart issue.

In light of everything that's been said about worshiping in truth, let's commit to expressing ourselves in a way that pleases the Father, and if we aren't there yet, let's recognize that this is a work in progress, and we need to keep pressing forward.

Here's a closing thought: often, *our* idea of a successful church service and *God's* idea are two different things. While we may be concerned with how everything looks and sounds outwardly, God is much more concerned with whether His people are worshiping with true integrity!

Summation

1. To worship in truth is to worship with integrity of heart—having a heart that is pure and undivided.
2. To worship in truth is to worship with integrity of mind—thinking in our minds what we are saying with our lips.
3. To worship in truth is to worship with integrity of speech—letting our "yes" *mean* yes and our "no" *mean* no! What we

sing during times of praise and worship should be consistent with what we really *mean* and *do*.

Devotional Exercises

1. As you are involved in praise and worship over the next few weeks, pay close attention to how well your words match up to what is going on in your heart and mind. Are you *feeling in your heart* and *thinking in your mind* what you are *saying with your lips*?
2. Consciously monitor your speech over the next few weeks. Are there instances where people might devalue the integrity of your word? In other words:
    - Have you made promises you didn't keep?
    - Have you said things you didn't really mean?

Study Guide Questions—Chapter 7

1. In your own words, what does it mean to worship with integrity of heart?
2. List some ways a person might be worshiping with an impure or divided heart.
3. In your own words, what does it mean to worship with integrity of mind?
4. Explain how Isaiah 29:13 applies to modern-day worship services.
5. In your own words, what does it mean to worship with integrity of speech?
6. Give some examples of your congregation singing something, but not acting in a manner that's consistent with what's being sung.
7. If the church would practice integrity of heart, mind, and speech among believers and unbelievers alike, what kind of impact do you think this would have on our community… our region… our world?

Chapter 8

THE PRACTICE OF PRAISE: WORSHIPING IN TRUTH

Part 3

In this chapter, we will further explore the concept of worshiping in truth.

Remember, in chapter 6, we learned that worshiping God in truth means we engage in a living interaction with Him, according to the pattern set forth in His Word; various expressions in the Old and New Testaments serve as important parameters for how we can and should express ourselves today.

Similarly, in chapter 7, we considered the importance of worshiping with integrity of heart, mind, and speech.

In this chapter, we will study the *true meaning* of biblical words for praise and worship, so we can align our worship patterns more consistently with biblical intent.

Before diving into what the Old and New Testaments specifically say, let me point out that the Old Testament provides numerous concrete examples of praise and worship expression, while the New Testament is somewhat (but not entirely) silent on the issue. While the Old Testament outlines several physical forms, the New Testament plainly instructs us to love the Lord with all our heart, soul, mind, and *strength*. Here are a couple observations:

1. In the same way the Old Testament outlines ten detailed commandments, and the New Testament sums these up in two statements (love the Lord and love your neighbor), so the Old Testament provides numerous physical forms for praise, which are summed up in the statement, "Love the Lord with all your *strength*" (which requires a physical response).
2. In the same way we do not throw out the Ten Commandments of the Old Testament, so the physical forms of praise and worship found therein should be valued and implemented in our modern-day worship services.

So, let's study specific words and meanings, but in doing so, we should keep in mind the overarching theme of worshiping the Lord with all our *strength*.

There is a wide gap between twenty-first-century English and biblical Greek and Hebrew. Both Greek and Hebrew are much more picturesque than English, and, very often, one Greek or Hebrew word represents a concept so multifaceted, that it almost defies English definition. Let's build upon the resolution that we should worship biblically, and in doing so, let's study what the Bible really *means* in original languages.

For example, if you study the Hebrew word *guwl,* translated "rejoice," in the last part of Zephaniah 3:17, you find that it actually means "to spin around under the influence of any violent (a.k.a., fervent) emotion."[15] This is what the prophet Zephaniah declared the Lord does when He rejoices over His people! The picture here is not of a stuffy old man, concerned with preserving his dignity or propriety; rather, we see a passionate Father, whose love for His people is so overwhelming that He can't stand still (as a bridegroom

---

[15] *Guwl* (Strong's Hb1523) as defined in *A Concise Dictionary of the Words in the Hebrew Bible with Their Renderings in the Authorized English Version* (Nashville, TN: Abingdon Press, 1973), 27; cross reference—Isaiah 62:5, expounded upon in *Isaiah: The NIV Application Commentary* by John N. Oswalt (Grand Rapids, MI: Zondervan, 2003), 655–56.

longs for his bride). He actually breaks forth into song and circles about with great joy!

(Side note: This example, where the Father actually rejoices/sings over His people, is also referred to as the song of the Lord. In scripture, the Father, at times, ministers to His people with songs of encouragement, deliverance, etc.)

Greek References to Worship

As stated previously, the New Testament gives relatively few concrete, physical expressions of praise and worship, though we see evidence of musical expression throughout its pages. Consider songs of the Savior's birth in Luke; hymns of the apostles; psalms, hymns, and spiritual songs alluded to in Ephesians and Colossians; and the numerous songs of Revelation.

The word most often translated "worship" in the New Testament is *proskuneo,* which means "to kiss the hand toward; to bow oneself in humble adoration."[16] As you can see, this definition denotes *intimacy* and *humility*, two very important qualities one would find in biblical praise and worship (though you wouldn't necessarily see this, reading the word "worship" in your English Bible).

Hebrew References to Worship

In the Old Testament, particularly the book of Psalms, we find numerous physical expressions of praise and worship. In some instances, our English translations have done a fairly good job of capturing the essence of such expressions.

For instance, the Hebrew word *ruwa* is often translated "joyful noise" and encompasses a variety of audible expressions of exuberant

---

16 *Proskuneo* (Strong's *Gk4352*) as defined in *A Concise Dictionary of the Words in the Greek Testament with Their Renderings in the Authorized English Version* (Nashville, TN: Abingdon Press, 1973), 61; and as expounded upon in *The New International Dictionary of New Testament Theology*, edited by Colin Brown (Grand Rapids, MI: Zondervan, 1971), 2:875–78.

praise.[17] In our culture, this could include a shout, a whistle, applause. In my opinion, even a high five would qualify. Sound strange? Well, consider the typical football game—the deafening roar of thousands of fans stomping their feet on bleachers or cheering loudly when the wide receiver makes a touchdown. Please don't misunderstand. Our God is an awesome God, and there are times when manifestations of His presence are such that complete silence and reverential awe is the only appropriate response. But we must be careful not to associate loud noise with disrespect. Jesus had the perfect opportunity to set the record straight during His triumphal procession into Jerusalem. (See Luke 19:37–40.) The people were involving themselves in rejoicing and *ruwa*-ing, to the point that religious leaders were disgusted and told Jesus to silence the clamor. Easily, Jesus could have straightened out the worshipers' theology and motioned for silence. Instead, though, He encouraged the clamor and stated that the rocks and stones would cry out if the people were silent!

> Luke 19:37–40: "When he came near the place where the road goes down the Mount of Olives, the whole crowd of disciples began joyfully to praise God in loud voices for all the miracles they had seen: 'Blessed is the king who comes in the name of the Lord!' 'Peace in heaven and glory in the highest!' Some of the Pharisees in the crowd said to Jesus, 'Teacher, rebuke your disciples!' 'I tell you,' he replied, 'if they keep quiet, the stones will cry out.'"

The truth is, there are times when silence is our only appropriate response, but there are also times when loud expressions of exceeding joy are the most appropriate way we can honor our victorious, triumphant King! So next time you are in a service and someone shouts or whistles, understand that there is solid biblical precedent for such expression. In making this point, let me stress the importance of every worshiper involving his or her *heart*, whatever the joyful noise. In particular, clapping, the most common joyful noise in many churches today, can be very trite and empty unless the worshiper truly engages his or her heart.

---

[17] *Ruwa* (Strong's Hb7321) as defined in *A Concise Dictionary of the Words in the Hebrew Bible with Their Renderings in the Authorized English Version* (Nashville, TN: Abingdon Press, 1973), 107; and as expounded upon in *The New Brown-Driver-Briggs Hebrew-English Lexicon* by Francis Brown, S. R. Driver, and Charles A. Briggs (Peabody, MA: Hendrickson, 1979), 929.

Other instances where English translations have captured the essence of particular expressions include references to singing (*ranan*) and dancing (*machowl*).

Ranan[18] is used in passages such as Psalm 67:4:

"May the nations be glad and sing [*ranan*] for joy, for you rule the peoples justly and guide the nations of the earth" (NIV).

"O let the nations be glad and sing [*ranan*] for joy: for thou shalt judge the people righteously, and govern the nations upon earth" (KJV).

Machowl[19] is used in passages such as Psalm 30:11:

"You turned my wailing into dancing [*machowl*]; you removed my sackcloth and clothed me with joy" (NIV).

"Thou hast turned for me my mourning into dancing [*machowl*]: thou hast put off my sackcloth, and girded me with gladness" (KJV).

Sometimes, we encounter synonyms for praise, such as "magnify" and "extol." Looking at such words in original Hebrew opens our eyes to a lot of hidden meaning. For example, the Hebrew word *gadal* is often translated "magnify" and actually means "to make large," which lends to the idea of every surrounding thing becoming smaller.[20] The picture we have, then, is the Lord becoming large in our sight while circumstances become smaller, or diminish in importance. (See Psalm 34:3.)

Similarly, the Hebrew word *ruwm* is often translated "extol" and

---

[18] *Ranan* (Strong's Hb7442) as defined in *Hebrew to English Index—Lexicon of the NIV Exhaustive Concordance* by Edward Goodrick and John R. Kohlenberger III (Grand Rapids, MI: Zondervan, 1990), 1618.

[19] *Machowl* (Strong's Hb4234) as appearing in *A Concise Dictionary of the Words in the Hebrew Bible with Their Renderings in the Authorized English Version* (Nashville, TN: Abingdon Press, 1973), 64.

[20] *Gadal* (Strong's Hb1431) as defined in *A Concise Dictionary of the Words in the Hebrew Bible with Their Renderings in the Authorized English Version* (Nashville, TN: Abingdon Press, 1973), 26; and as expounded upon in *Theological Wordbook of the Old Testament*, edited by R. Laird Harris, Gleason L. Archer Jr., and Bruce K. Waltke (Chicago: Moody Press, 1980), 1:151.

actually means "to be lifted up; to be high."[21] This form of praise is often used in portions of scripture where worshipers are recognizing the King's rightful position of supremacy, through acts of reverence such as bowing one's head or standing in honor. (See Psalm 30:1.)

> Psalm 34:3: "O magnify [*gadal*] the Lord with me, and let us exalt his name together" (KJV).
>
> Psalm 30:1: "I will exalt [*ruwm*] you, O Lord, for you lifted me out of the depths and did not let my enemies gloat over me" (NIV).

We would not typically see such shades of meaning without moving past limited English translations and seeing exactly what the original languages say.

Seven Hebrew Words for Praise

Finally, in our English Bibles, we see the word "praise" hundreds of times. The incredible thing is that there are several different Hebrew words translated "praise" in our English Bibles, and the different words mean very different things! Settling for the translation "praise" would be like describing artwork to a blind man by simply calling everything a "picture," making no distinction between *color* or *black and white, birds flying over a beautiful sunset,* or *a bowl of fruit on a rough-hewn oak table.*

What a sad thought! The man would have no appreciation for the distinct differences between modern art and the masterpieces of the Renaissance. Michelangelo's painting on the ceiling of the Sistine Chapel would be equated, in the blind man's eyes, to an eight-by-ten Kodak photo from your last family vacation! If the blind man could only see, he would discover the truth that all pictures aren't created equal.

In the same way, we, God's people, have been blind to the richness of praise and worship for many years—dependent upon the weakness of our English vocabulary to capture the true essence of praise and worship expression. We must understand that each time the word "praise" appears in the Bible, it doesn't always mean the same thing,

---

[21] *Ruwm* (Strong's Hb7311) as defined in *A Concise Dictionary of the Words in the Hebrew Bible with Their Renderings in the Authorized English Version* (Nashville, TN: Abingdon Press, 1973), 107.

but actually represents a variety of distinct expressions! As this lesson concludes, let's look at seven of the most common Hebrew words for praise, those found particularly in the book of Psalms, and in doing so, let's discover a richer understanding of their meanings.

1. *Halal*: "To shine forth, celebrate, rave, boast, make a show, be hilarious or clamorously foolish."[22]

1 Chronicles 16:4: "He appointed some of the Levites to minister before the ark of the LORD, to make petition, to give thanks, and to praise [*halal*] the LORD, the God of Israel" (NIV).

Psalm 22:22: "I will declare your name to my brothers; in the congregation I will praise [*halal*] you" (NIV).

Psalm 35:18: "I will give you thanks in the great assembly; among throngs of people I will praise [*halal*] you" (NIV).

Psalm 149:3: "Let them praise [*halal*] his name with dancing and make music to him with tambourine and harp" (NIV).

Psalm 150:1: "Praise [*halal*] the LORD. Praise [*halal*] God in his sanctuary; praise [*halal*] him in his mighty heavens" (NIV).

Halal is the most common word for "praise," but unfortunately, it is often the least practiced expression in the church. Our English word "hallelujah" is derived from *halal.*

2. *Shabach*: "To address in a loud tone, to commend, to glory, to triumph in praise."[23]

---

[22] *Halal* (Strong's Hb1984) as defined in *A Concise Dictionary of the Words in the Hebrew Bible with Their Renderings in the Authorized English Version* (Nashville, TN: Abingdon Press, 1973), 33.

[23] *Shabach* (Strong's Hb7623) as defined in *A Concise Dictionary of the Words in the Hebrew Bible with Their Renderings in the Authorized English Version* (Nashville, TN: Abingdon Press, 1973), 111.

Psalm 63:3: "Because thy lovingkindness is better than life, my lips shall praise [*shabach*] thee" (KJV).

Psalm 117:1: "O praise the LORD, all ye nations: praise [*shabach*] him, all ye people" (KJV).

Psalm 145:4: "One generation shall praise [*shabach*] thy works to another, and shall declare thy mighty acts" (KJV).

A lot of popular sources associate *shabach* with the victory shout, but it is better translated "loud praise." *Ruwa*, the word for "joyful noise" mentioned earlier in this chapter, actually means "to shout as a victor triumphs in battle."[24]

3. *Barak*: "To kneel, to congratulate or bless from a humble position."[25]

In addition to its obvious use in passages such as Psalm 95:6, (which says, "Come, let us *bow down* in worship, let us *kneel* before the LORD our Maker"), *barak* is also simply translated "praise" as follows:

Judges 5:2: "When the princes in Israel take the lead, when the people willingly offer themselves—praise [*barak*] the Lord!" (NIV).

Psalm 68:26: "Praise [*barak*] God in the great congregation; praise the LORD in the assembly of Israel" (NIV).

Psalm 103:1: "Praise [*barak*] the LORD, O my soul; all my inmost being, praise [*barak*] his holy name" (NIV).

---

24 *Ruwa* (Strong's Hb7321) as defined in *The New Brown-Driver-Briggs-Gesenius Hebrew and English Lexicon* (Peabody, MA: Hendrickson, 1979), 929. See Joshua 6:16, Psalm 47:1, etc.

25 *Barak* (Strong's Hb1288) as defined in *A Concise Dictionary of the Words in the Hebrew Bible with Their Renderings in the Authorized English Version* (Nashville, TN: Abingdon Press, 1973), 24.

4. *Zamar*: "To touch upon the strings, to play upon a musical instrument."[26]

Psalm 21:13: "Be exalted, O Lord, in your strength; we will sing and praise [*zamar*] your might" (NIV).

Psalm 57:7: "My heart is fixed, O God, my heart is fixed: I will sing and give praise [*zamar*]" (KJV).

Psalm 108:1: "O God, my heart is fixed; I will sing and give praise [*zamar*], even with my glory" (KJV).

Psalm 138:1: "I will praise [*zamar*] you, O LORD, with all my heart; before the 'gods' I will sing your praise" (NIV).

5. *Towdah*: "To extend the hands, specifically as a sacrifice of thanksgiving."[27]

Psalm 42:4: "When I remember these things, I pour out my soul in me: for I had gone with the multitude, I went with them to the house of God, with the voice of joy and praise [*towdah*], with a multitude that kept holy days" (KJV).

Psalm 50:23: "Whoso offereth praise [*towdah*] glorifieth me: and to him that ordereth his conversation aright will I show the salvation of God" (KJV).

Jeremiah 33:10–11: "Thus saith the LORD: Again there shall be heard in this place ... the voice of joy, and the voice of gladness, the voice of the bridegroom, and the voice of the bride ... and of them

---

[26] *Zamar* (Strong's Hb2167) as defined in *A Concise Dictionary of the Words in the Hebrew Bible with Their Renderings in the Authorized English Version* (Nashville, TN: Abingdon Press, 1973), 35.

[27] *Towdah* (Strong's Hb8426) as defined in *A Concise Dictionary of the Words in the Hebrew Bible with Their Renderings in the Authorized English Version* (Nashville, TN: Abingdon Press, 1973), 123.

that shall bring the sacrifice of praise [*towdah*] into the house of the LORD" (KJV).

6. *Yadah*: "To extend the hand or hands, by an act of the will, usually as an expression of reverence."[28]

2 Chronicles 20:21: "And when he had consulted with the people, he appointed singers unto the LORD, and that should praise the beauty of holiness, as they went out before the army, and to say, 'Praise [*yadah*] the LORD; for his mercy endureth forever'" (KJV).

Psalm 9:1: "I will praise [*yadah*] thee, O LORD, with my whole heart; I will show forth all thy marvelous works" (KJV).

Psalm 107:8: "Oh that men would praise [*yadah*] the LORD for his goodness, and for his wonderful works to the children of men!" (KJV).

Psalm 145:10: "All you have made will praise [*yadah*] you, O LORD; your saints will extol you" (NIV).

Isaiah 12:4: "In that day shall ye say, Praise [*yadah*] the LORD, call upon his name, declare his doings among the people, make mention that his name is exalted" (KJV).

Though *yadah* and *towdah* are very similar, in that they both indicate the extension of the hands, there is a distinctly different focus of the heart and mind *as* the hands are extended:

Yadah may reflect reverence as we sing: "I stand, I stand in awe of you" or "I love you, Lord, and I lift my voice," whereas…

Towdah might reflect a sacrifice of thanksgiving as we declare:

---

[28] *Yadah* (Strong's Hb3034) as defined in *A Concise Dictionary of the Words in the Hebrew Bible with Their Renderings in the Authorized English Version* (Nashville, TN: Abingdon Press, 1973), 47.

"With a heart of thanksgiving, I will bless thee, O Lord," or "Thank you, Lord; I just want to thank you."

Let me take a moment to further explain the significance of lifting our hands. The expression may reflect reverence or thanksgiving, as we've already seen, but let's also consider the following:

1. The posture exemplifies a child reaching out to Daddy God, in a state of dependence and vulnerability.
2. The posture is an outward symbol of surrender, as worshipers are relinquishing control to God and allowing Him to have His way.

Lifting your hands may seem foreign or culturally out of place, but keep in mind that God had good reason for wanting people to express themselves in this way. There is a purpose behind the expression.

7. *Tehillah*: "To sing a song from the heart."[29]

Psalm 34:1: "I will extol the LORD at all times; his praise [*tehillah*] will always be on my lips" (NIV).

Psalm 40:3: "He put a new song in my mouth, a hymn of praise [*tehillah*] to our God. Many will see and fear and put their trust in the LORD" (NIV).

Psalm 71:8: "My mouth is filled with your praise [*tehillah*], declaring your splendor all day long" (NIV).

---

[29] *Tehillah* (Strong's Hb8416) as defined in *A Concise Dictionary of the Words in the Hebrew Bible with Their Renderings in the Authorized English Version* (Nashville, TN: Abingdon Press, 1973), 123; and as expounded upon in *The International Standard Bible Encyclopedia*, Vol. 3, revised edition (Grand Rapids, MI: William B. Eerdmans, 1995), 930. Scriptural examples of *tehillah* as a song rising out of the heart, often spontaneously, include Psalm 9:14; 22:25; 34:1; 35:28; 40:3; 51:15; 71:6, 8, 14; 106:12; 119:171; 145:21; 149:1; and Isaiah 42:10; 43:21; 61:3, 11.

Psalm 149:1: "Praise the Lord. Sing to the Lord a new song, his praise [*tehillah*] in the assembly of the saints" (NIV).

Isaiah 42:10: "Sing to the Lord a new song, his praise [*tehillah*] from the ends of the earth, you who go down to the sea, and all that is in it, you islands, and all who live in them" (NIV).

Isaiah 61:3: "To bestow on them a crown of beauty instead of ashes, the oil of gladness instead of mourning, and a garment of praise [*tehillah*] instead of a spirit of despair. They will be called oaks of righteousness, a planting of the LORD for the display of his splendor" (NIV).

During a time of praise and worship, you will hear this expression when the congregation is singing heartfelt songs to the Lord. But I believe there is more to *tehillah* than simply singing the average worship song. As we take a look at several verses that utilize this word, it appears that *tehillah* is a special type of song, one that is birthed from deep within, often a spontaneous expression born during times of adversity. Chapter 9 will be devoted solely to this aspect of praise and worship, and as we will discover, *tehillah* is one of the most personal and intimate expressions we could offer to the Lord.

It's my hope that this brief study has inspired you to dig a little deeper—to see what God's Word really says about praise and worship expression. I'm sure you can tell we've only scratched the surface. There's so much more to discover, so study on!

Summation

1. To worship in truth is to worship according to the patterns set forth in the Word of God.
2. To understand the true nature of biblical praise and worship, we must recognize the distinctions between various Greek and Hebrew words used in scripture.
3. Reverential silence and exuberant rejoicing are both appropriate responses, in proper season, as we praise and worship the Lord.

4. Whatever the expression, the worshiper must engage his or her heart.

Devotional Exercises

1. Over the next few weeks, consciously experiment with each of the seven Hebrew words for praise mentioned in this lesson. Note your feelings as you step out with expression. What is happening in your spirit? Do the different expressions feel different? Which is easier to demonstrate, which is harder, and why?
2. Read a few psalms and try to guess which Hebrew word is being used when you read the word "praise" in your English Bible.
3. In corporate times of praise and worship, as "praise" appears in the lyrics of songs we're singing, try and figure out which Hebrew word(s) might be most appropriate, based on context.

Study Guide Questions—Chapter 8

1. Read the words to each of the seven songs below. Indicate a Hebrew word (expression) for "praise" that might be most appropriate, based on context. Then, explain *why* a particular word has been chosen. (Use each word only once.)

"Revelation Song"
Worthy is the Lamb Who was slain
Holy, holy is He
Sing a new song to Him Who sits on
Heaven's mercy seat

Holy, holy, holy is the Lord God Almighty
Who was and is and is to come
With all creation I sing *praise* to the King of kings
You are my everything, and I will adore You

Copyright 2004 Gateway Create Publishing

"Ever Be"

Your love is devoted like a ring of solid gold
Like a vow that is tested, like a covenant of old
Your love is enduring through the winter rain
And beyond the horizon with mercy for today
Faithful You have been and faithful You will be
You pledge Yourself to me, and it's why I sing

Your *praise* will ever be on my lips, ever be on my lips
Your *praise* will ever be on my lips, ever be on my lips
(REPEAT)

You will be *praised*, You will be *praised*
With angels and saints we sing, "Worthy are You, Lord!"
(REPEAT)

Copyright 2014 Bethel Music Publishing

"I Will Bless the Lord"

Mender of the broken, Healer of the soul
Redeemer of all yesterdays, oh I will bless You Lord
Maker of the heavens, the oceans and the skies
All the earth rejoices, it's You we glorify

I will bless the Lord, I will bless the Lord
At all times, at all times

I will bless You, Lord, Your *praise* will always be
Forever in my mouth, forever on my lips

Copyright 2009 Miami Life Sounds Publishing, Inc.

"Turn It Up"

You are here as we lift You up
You are riding on our *praise*
Be enthroned over everything
You are seated in our *praise*
This is prophetic, I can feel it in the air
We lift our *praise* and You change the atmosphere
With hearts open now, everybody singing out "oh"

Turn it up, this sound of *praise*
Make it louder than any other
Lift Him up and shout His name over all

Our *praise* goes up, Your rain comes down
(REPEAT)

Copyright 2012 Planetshakers Ministries Int., Inc.

"Walls"

We are daughters and sons, singing as one
We've got a hope now
Walls have tried to divide, but nothing can hide
The power that we found
You are walking with us, and all of the walls are turning to dust
They are falling down

Sing *praise*, we sing *praise*
We fill the skies with song from our hearts
Sing *praise*, we sing *praise*
Till enemies know how faithful You are, oh God

Walls are coming down, walls are coming down, oh, oh

Copyright 2015 Dayspring Music, LLC and Gateway Create Publishing

"From the Inside Out"

A thousand times I've failed, still Your mercy remains
And should I stumble again, still I'm caught in Your grace
Everlasting, Your light will shine when all else fades
Never-ending, Your glory goes beyond all fame
Your will above all else, my purpose remains
The art of losing myself in bringing You *praise*
Everlasting, Your light will shine when all else fades
Never-ending, Your glory goes beyond all fame

My heart and my soul, I give You control
Consume me from the inside out, Lord
Let justice and *praise* become my embrace
To love You from the inside out

Everlasting, Your light will shine when all else fades
Never-ending, Your glory goes beyond all fame
And the cry of my heart is to bring You *praise*
From the inside out, Lord, my soul cries out

Copyright 2005 Hillsong Music Publishing

"Endless Praise"
You are God, and we lift You up
We'll keep singing, we'll keep praising
We won't stop giving all we got
'Cause You're worthy of all glory
Oh, there is no other, You are forever Lord over all
There's nobody like You, no one beside You

To You let endless *praise* resound
Every night and day, and with no delay
Let endless *praise* resound

We lift You up, up, up
We're giving You our love, love, love
For everything You've done, done, done
We give You all the *praise*

Copyright 2012 Planetshakers Ministries Int., Inc.

2. What has been the greatest thing you've learned from chapters 6, 7, and 8 (worshiping in truth)?

SET LIST EXERCISES

Directions:

1. For each set list provided, describe the interaction taking place between God and the worshiper.
2. Chart the progression, from the outer court, through the holy place, and into the holy of holies.
3. List biblical references and/or scriptural principles found in each song.
4. Indicate which Hebrew expression(s) of "praise" would be most appropriate for each song.

(Use a separate sheet of paper if necessary.)

Worship service
November 30, 2014

"Nothing Is Impossible"
"One Thing Remains"
"I Call You Jesus"
"I Worship You, Almighty God"
"Great I Am"

"Nothing Is Impossible"
I'm not gonna live by what I see
I'm not gonna live by what I feel
Deep down I know that You're here with me
And I know that You can do anything
Through You, I can do anything
I can do all things 'cause it's You Who gives me strength
Nothing is impossible
Through You blind eyes are open
Strongholds are broken, I am living by faith
Nothing is impossible
I believe, I believe
I believe, I believe in You

Copyright 2008 Integrity Music Publishing and Planetshakers Ministries Int., Inc.

"One Thing Remains"

Higher than the mountains that I face
Stronger than the power of the grave
Constant through the trial and the change
One thing remains, one thing remains
Your love never fails, it never gives up, never runs out on me
On and on and on and on it goes
It overwhelms and satisfies my soul
And I never, ever have to be afraid
One thing remains, one thing remains
In death, in life I'm confident and covered by the power
Of Your great love
My debt is paid, there's nothing that can separate my heart
From Your great love

Copyright 2010 ChristaJoy Music Publishing, Bethel Music Publishing, and Vineyard Music USA

"I Call You Jesus"

Healer, Mender, Master, Savior
Lover, Giver, Name above all names
Ruler, Redeemer, Risen Conqueror
Jesus, Jesus, Name above all names
Your name is Jesus, risen from the dead
You are the glory, the lifter of our head
You have the only name by which we can be saved
I call You Jesus, oh, oh, I call You Jesus, oh, oh
Nobody greater than You, nobody stronger than You
No name is higher than the name of Jesus
Nobody bigger than You, no one can do what You do
No name is higher than the name of, higher than the name of Jesus

Copyright 2012 Integrity's Praise! Music, Planetshakers Ministries Int., Inc., and Sound of the New Breed

"I Worship You, Almighty God"

I worship You, Almighty God, there is none like You
I worship You, oh Prince of Peace, that is what I want to do
I give You praise, for You are my righteousness
I worship You, Almighty God, there is none like You

Copyright 1983 Integrity's Hosanna! Music

"Great I Am"
I wanna be close, close to Your side
So heaven is real and death is a lie
I wanna hear voices of angels above singing as one
Hallelujah, holy, holy, God Almighty, Great I Am
Who is worthy, none beside Thee, God Almighty, Great I Am
The mountains shake before You, the demons run and flee
At the mention of Your name, King of Majesty
There is no pow'r in hell or any who can stand
Before the power and the presence of the Great I Am
The Great I Am

Copyright 2011 Integrity Music Publishing

Worship service
March 23, 2008

"He's Worthy"
"Let Us Adore"
"Revelation Song"
"All Honor"
"Amazed"

"He's Worthy"
I'm making my declaration, I'm shouting it to ev'ry nation
I bless the God of my salvation He's worthy, worthy
The God I serve is great and mighty
He is for me, who can be against me
I praise Him with a song of vict'ry He's worthy, worthy
I will bless and glorify His Name
No other name is worthy to be praised
He's worthy, He's worthy, He is worthy, bless His name
Let the nations rise and worship He who sits upon the throne
He is worthy of the glory, He and He alone

Copyright 2006 DaviShop and Integrity's Hosanna! Music

"Let Us Adore"

The heavens declare the glory of God
And all of the world will join the praise, His wonders proclaim
The oceans and skies lift up their voice
And all He has made will rise to bless the King of all kings
Let us adore Him, let us adore Him
Jesus Christ is the Lord
Come and behold Him, bow down before Him
Jesus Christ is the Lord
Hallelujah, hallelujah, You are worthy of all praise

Copyright 2005 Hillsong Music Publishing

"Revelation Song"

Worthy is the Lamb Who was slain
Holy, holy is He
Sing a new song to Him Who sits on
Heaven's mercy seat
Holy, holy, holy is the Lord God Almighty
Who was and is and is to come
With all creation I sing praise to the King of kings
You are my ev'rything, and I will adore You

Copyright 2004 Gateway Create Publishing

"All Honor"

All honor, all glory be unto You
They belong to You
All wisdom, all power flow from Your throne
They are Yours alone
All glory to Your name, for wondrous are Your ways
In majesty You reign, for You are holy
And all the earth will sing, proclaim You Lord and King
They'll come and bow their knee, for You are holy
All the earth proclaim that You are holy

Copyright 2004 Belden Street Music Publishing

"Amazed"

You dance over me while I am unaware
You sing all around, but I never hear the sound
Lord, I'm amazed by You
Lord, I'm amazed by You
Lord, I'm amazed by You
How You love me
How deep, how wide, how great
Is Your love for me

Copyright 2004 Integrity Music Publishing

Chapter 9

THE PERSONALITY OF PRAISE: HEART SONGS TO THE LORD

At the end of chapter 8, we discussed seven Hebrew words for praise. Each was distinct in its meaning and expression. In this chapter, we will explore the seventh word in greater detail.

As I said, I believe *tehillah* is the most intimate expression of praise and worship. Let's take a little time to back that statement up and then move on to some practical instruction in the development of this expression for our private and public praise and worship.

When we release spontaneous expressions of praise and worship from our spirits, we are engaging in the most personal communication possible. The songs are expressed through the uniqueness of our personality and current relationship/walk with God. Furthermore, these heart songs best illustrate and express our love relationship with Abba Father, as we align ourselves with the Spirit and Mind of God. (*Abba* is a Hebrew term of endearment, meaning "Daddy God.")

This chapter will focus on three English terms that are often used to denote the idea of expressing heart songs, although the terms are not necessarily identical. All three *do* allude to the idea of singing in the Spirit, or free, open worship. With this type of expression, musicians typically provide an instrumental underscore, over which other instruments and voices of the congregation create new melodies spontaneously. This personality of praise is beautiful corporately (like the sound of many waters John describes in Revelation), but at the same time, it is very personal, as each individual expresses his or her song to the Lord in a way that it is distinguished from the rest of the group.

Keeping all of this in mind, let's explore the three terms, one at a time.

1. Spiritual Songs (*ode* in Greek)[30]

In Ephesians and Colossians, it appears that *spiritual songs should be a regular part of personal and corporate praise and worship times.* (See the scriptures below.) Balanced praise and worship should be made up of three types of songs. In most churches, we readily find psalms (scriptural choruses, possibly derived from the book of Psalms) and hymns (works of human composition that unpack doctrine or weightier matters of the faith). The third type, spiritual songs, is a bit rarer, which is a problem if we want to have a healthy worship diet. Including psalms and hymns during times of praise and worship, at the absence of spiritual songs, is like eating meats and carbs without ever partaking of essential fruits and veggies. I would contend that most Western churches do not have a very "balanced" worship diet, and thus, the need for this chapter!

> Ephesians 5:17–19: "Therefore do not be foolish, but understand what the Lord's will is. Do not get drunk on wine, which leads to debauchery. Instead, be filled with the Spirit. Speak to one another with psalms, hymns and spiritual songs. Sing and make music in [with] your heart to the Lord."
>
> Colossians 3:16: "Let the word of Christ dwell in you richly as you teach and admonish one another with all wisdom, and as you sing psalms, hymns and spiritual songs with gratitude in [with] your hearts to God."

Look again at Ephesians 5:17–19 and Colossians 3:16 to the left, and notice the following: the melody is made "by" or "with" the heart—not just "in" the heart. Like we've

[30] *Ode* (Strong's *Gk5603*): a free-form song, supernatural in its origin, as defined in *Greek-English Lexicon of the New Testament: Based on Semantic Domains*, electronic edition of the 2nd ed., by Johannes P. Louw and Eugene Albert Nida (New York: United Bible Societies, 1996), 33.110.

mentioned before, our English translations at times do not do justice to what the Bible really says in a particular passage. The word translated "in" is the Greek word *ev*, which can be defined as "in, on, at, among, with, within, by, by means of, etc."[31] In this passage, *ev* refers to *how* something is accomplished, not *where* it is accomplished. So we are not referring to singing that happens internally—in someone's heart. We are instead referring to singing that happens with, or by means of, the heart, which translates into outward expression.

We also see in the Colossians passage that the Word of God is central in these songs: "Let the Word of God … dwell in you richly as you teach … *and* as you sing." Spiritual songs should be filled with scripture that we've placed in our hearts.

Finally, the Ephesians passage illustrates that spiritual songs are Spirit-induced: "Be filled with the Spirit [which will cause you to] speak to one another [and] sing and make music … to the Lord."

Concerning the last point, spiritual songs are not just created in the mind, though the mind will actively be engaged (or *should* be engaged). Spiritual songs are Spirit-led and Spirit-controlled. One should not suppose, though, that the Spirit takes over, and we uncontrollably begin to sing new songs. Singing new songs is accomplished as we engage our will and begin to speak/sing through the inspiration of the Holy Spirit.

Two distinct types of spiritual songs come to mind. There are spiritual songs for the individual and spiritual songs for the congregation. In the first, I sing a spontaneous, Spirit-led song to the Lord, for His enjoyment. In the second, I sing a spontaneous, Spirit-led song before the congregation, which brings encouragement and edification to the Body of Christ.

---

[31] *Ev* (Strong's *Gk1722*) as defined in *A Concise Dictionary of the Words in the Greek Testament with Their Renderings in the Authorized English Version* (Nashville, TN: Abingdon Press, 1973), 28.

2. New Songs

(sang = *shiyrah*[32] / song = *shuwr* in Hebrew[33])
(sang = *aido*[34] / song = *ode* in Greek[35])

There is a slightly different impromptu song that can be sung during times of praise and worship. Like spiritual songs, new songs are spontaneously developed, *but in a way that others can join in.* Consider the numerous examples below.

The people celebrated with the song of Moses and Miriam after God led them successfully through the Red Sea (Exodus 15:1–2)…

"Then Moses and the Israelites sang this song to the LORD: 'I will sing to the LORD, for he is highly exalted. The horse and its rider he has hurled into the sea. The LORD is my strength and my song; he has become my salvation. He is my God, and I will praise him; my father's God, and I will exalt him.'"

God promised his people water, and they sang a new song (Numbers 21:16–18)…

"From there they continued on to Beer, the well where the LORD said to Moses, 'Gather the people together and I will give them water.' Then Israel sang this song: 'Spring up, O well! Sing about it, about the well that the princes dug, that the nobles of the

---

32 *Shuwr* (Strong's Hb7891): to sing a melody that is intended to be sung by others; Greek equivalent *aido*, as defined in *Greek-English Lexicon of the New Testament: Based on Semantic Domains*, electronic edition of the 2nd ed., by Johannes P. Louw and Eugene Albert Nida (New York: United Bible Societies, 1996), 6.83–6.95.

33 *Shiyrah* (Strong's Hb7892): a song that uses the voice in a unique melodic and rhythmic manner; Greek equivalent *ode*, as defined in *Greek-English Lexicon of the New Testament: Based on Semantic Domains*, electronic edition of the 2nd ed., by Johannes P. Louw and Eugene Albert Nida (New York: United Bible Societies, 1996), 6.83–6.95.

34 *Ode* (Strong's *Gk5603*): a free-form song, supernatural in its origin, as defined in Louw and Nida (see #29 above).

35 *Aido* (Strong's *Gk103*): to make/sing a new melody, as defined in *Greek-English Lexicon of the New Testament: Based on Semantic Domains*, electronic edition of the 2nd ed., by Johannes P. Louw and Eugene Albert Nida (New York: United Bible Societies, 1996), 33.109.

people sank—the nobles with scepters and staffs.' Then they went from the desert to Mattanah."

The heavenly host, in worship around the throne, sings a new song (Revelation 5:9–14)...

"And they sang a new song: 'You are worthy to take the scroll and to open its seals, because you were slain, and with your blood you purchased men for God from every tribe and language and people and nation. You have made them to be a kingdom and priests to serve our God, and they will reign on the earth.' Then I looked and heard the voice of many angels, numbering thousands upon thousands, and ten thousand times ten thousand. They encircled the throne and the living creatures and the elders. In a loud voice they sang: 'Worthy is the Lamb, who was slain, to receive power and wealth and wisdom and strength and honor and glory and praise!' Then I heard every creature in heaven and on earth and under the earth and on the sea, and all that is in them, singing: 'To him who sits on the throne and to the Lamb be praise and honor and glory and power, forever and ever!' The four living creatures said, 'Amen,' and the elders fell down and worshiped."

The thing to keep in mind with all of these examples is that the people collectively began to join in the song as it developed spontaneously among them. What a powerful expression of praise and worship!

3. Heart Songs—*Tehillah*

Tehillah is the fourth-most-often-used word for "praise" in the Old Testament. It is a distinct type of song—the heart song—which makes it one of the most personal and authentic expressions possible because it arises out of the individual worshiper's heart.

Note some examples of *tehillah* to the right (Exodus 15:2, Psalm 22:3, and Psalm 147:1–2).

Exodus 15:2: "The LORD is my strength and my song; he has become my salvation. He is my God, and I will praise [*tehillah*] him; my father's God, and I will exalt him."

Psalm 22:3: "Yet you are enthroned as the Holy One; you are the praise [*tehillah*] of Israel."

Psalm 147:1–2: "Praise [*tehillah*] the LORD. How good it is to sing praises [*tehillah*] to our God, how pleasant and fitting to praise [*tehillah*] him! The LORD builds up Jerusalem; he gathers the exiles of Israel."

Also, God himself is our heart song, as depicted in Deuteronomy 10:21…

"He is your praise [*tehillah*]; he is your God, who performed for you those great and awesome wonders you saw with your own eyes."

My house will be called a house of heart songs?

At the cleansing of the temple, Jesus quoted Isaiah 56:7…

"These I will bring to my holy mountain and give them joy in my house of prayer. Their burnt offerings and sacrifices will be accepted on my altar; for my house will be called a house of prayer for all nations."

"Prayer" above is the Hebrew word *tephillah*, which looks a lot like *tehillah*, and in the strictest sense, means "prayer, plea, request, or petition."[36] What you may not realize, though, is that Hebrew prayers were most often *sung*, not spoken. Five of the psalms are actually called *tephillah* in their superscriptions,[37] and several other scriptures reference *tephillah* alongside singing and several of the postures of praise and worship referenced in the last chapter.

Jesus's insistence that the Father's house would be a house of "prayer" translates into the following: We need strong, heartfelt prayer *and singing* in the House of God! It's what He truly desires!

Here's something else He desires: an intimate, father-child relationship with us. As always, if you've grown up with a negative fatherly image, you will have to interpret that statement through the truth of God's Word, rather than allowing the filter of your past experience to taint this spiritual reality.

---

[36] *Tephillah* (Strong's Hb8605): prayer, worship, plea, request, or petition; Greek equivalent *proseuche* or *proseuchomai*, as defined in *Greek-English Lexicon of the New Testament: Based on Semantic Domains*, electronic edition of the 2nd ed., by Johannes P. Louw and Eugene Albert Nida (New York: United Bible Societies, 1996), 33.178 and 33.179; incidentally, Strong's defines *tephillah* as a hymn by implication.

[37] Psalms 17, 86, 90, 102, and 142 contain the word *tephillah* in their superscriptions. For examples of scriptures that contain *tephillah* alongside singing and worshipful postures, see 1 Kings 8:38, 54; 2 Chronicles 6:29; Psalm 42:8; Psalm 65:1–2; Psalm 141:2; and Isaiah 1:15.

Consider the following scripture…

"Those who are led by the Spirit of God are sons of God. For you did not receive a spirit that makes you a slave again to fear, but you received the Spirit of sonship. And by him we cry, 'Abba, Father'" (Romans 8:14–15).

Consider these additional scriptures, which illustrate that we are as children to our Heavenly Father…

"He called a little child and had him stand among them. And he said: 'I tell you the truth, unless you change and become like little children, you will never enter the kingdom of heaven. Therefore, whoever humbles himself like this child is the greatest in the kingdom of heaven'" (Matthew 18:2–4).

"How great is the love the Father has lavished on us, that we should be called children of God! And that is what we are! The reason the world does not know us is that it did not know him" (1 John 3:1).

Over and over again, believers are described as children or sons and daughters, and God is their loving Father.

Heart Songs or Hallmark

Now, let me illustrate the intimacy of heart songs in praise and worship, in relationship to this particular truth.

Most parents and grandparents have experienced the joy of receiving a homemade card or other piece of art from their children or grandchildren. Hallmark is nice, but there is something extra-special about receiving a card with stickmen, a blotchy yellow sun, and the words "I LUV U" almost unintelligibly scrawled on the inside. This card wins over Hallmark any day!

So consider this. The Lord is pleased when we sing hymns and choruses written by anointed men and women of God. *But there is something extraordinary about His children painting their own heart songs* upon the canvas of music, and with sincere hearts, offering those songs up to Daddy God, with all of their imperfections. We should paint pictures for Daddy often, so He can hang them up on the walls of heaven and show them off to His legions of angels!

With this in mind, let's move on to the practical.

David instructed his musicians and singers.

In 1 Chronicles 25:7, we read that King David, a worshiper after God's own heart, saw to it that his singers and musicians were properly developed and trained to minister before the Lord. Though it is possible to be so dependent upon skill and talent that the Holy Spirit is left out of the picture, it is equally possible that skill development and proper instruction are written off as unspiritual; in doing so, though, we actually hinder what the Spirit wants to do in us and through us.

It would be improper for you to gather a group of musicians together and, in the name of instruction, tell them that God is going to show up if they play every note perfectly. On the other hand, it would be just as improper for you to put a trumpet in someone's hands who has never played, send him to the platform, and tell him, "Just follow the Spirit, brother!"

Should the preacher "just trust the Spirit" and never study to show himself approved—or refuse to work on his delivery style because that aspect of his preaching ministry is unspiritual? Of course not! The preacher does the best he can to prepare, then lays it all at the feet of Jesus and submits everything to the Holy Spirit. In the same way, the worship leader rehearses with his or her team, in order to minister with excellence and adequately prepare for the Spirit's leading.

Lack of instruction and slothful preparation is *not* the answer. Good instruction and thorough preparation, fully submitted to dependence on the Holy Spirit, *is*!

Before we bring this lesson to a close, I want to give you some practical instruction in releasing heart songs—to equip you with a basic understanding of music, so you can begin to explore heart songs in your personal and corporate praise and worship times.

Someone may object—*"I don't have an ear for music..."* Well, I think we've already established that this isn't about being a singer or musician; it's about offering oneself wholly to the Lord, in the way He desires. God wants us to express our devotion to Him in song, clearly demonstrated in previous lessons.

Someone else may object—*"You can't teach an old dog new tricks..."*

Well, we're not dogs, and as children of God, we always need to be growing and moving forward! Also, heart songs aren't a "new" style of praise and worship, but really they get back to what God originally intended. Finally, this whole thing isn't a "trick," but, rather, the heart of God for His people—a biblical pattern for them to engage in.

Three basic song elements: Music, Lyrics, and Theme

Music

Music consists primarily of three things: melody (how pitches move up and down), tempo (how fast or slow the song is), and beat (or rhythm).

Lyrics

Song lyrics are simply the words used when one sings. An instrumental song only utilizes musical instruments and has no lyrics. Often, different people author the lyrics and music of a given song.

Theme

All songs depict at least one theme, or general idea. The theme can usually be detected by glancing at the lyrics. Ask yourself what message the words are trying to communicate. Also, the melody may reinforce the theme. For example, a happy theme may be characterized by happy-sounding music. A serious theme might be reinforced with sober-sounding melodies, etc.

The Creation of Heart Songs

Most often, heart songs flow from a theme that the Holy Spirit is currently impressing upon an individual or group. Remember the various pathways of the river of praise and worship—exaltation, celebration, warfare, intercession, etc.? These pathways can actually become the theme of your heart songs!

So as you move down a particular pathway, you have music and lyrics at your disposal, to create limitless new songs of praise and worship from your heart. However, just as an artist must become familiar with his brush, paints, and technique, you will have to do the same. Singing heart songs is an art that can be developed and improved upon as you mature in spontaneous praise and worship. Remember, as with the child's imperfect card, it doesn't matter how well you sing; rather, what matters is the love and sincerity with which you "paint" your heart songs to the Lord!

The Canvas, the Paint, and the Brush

For most, the musical underscore (or basic chord progression played by the band) functions as the "canvas" upon which you will paint your song. The "paint" is the words of your heart. The "brush" is the tool you use to get the paint from your heart onto the canvas. For singers (and most members of the congregation), voice is the primary brush used. Other parts of the body may add dimension, such as hands, feet, etc. For musicians, the brush can be their instrument, as they play from their heart, adding agreement to what's literally being spoken.

Let's Paint!

A painter, holding his palate of colors and gazing upon a blank canvas, is faced with incredible opportunity. In the same way, a worshiper of the Lord stands before Him, with unlimited possibility!

Here are some common methods of painting heart songs.

1. New lyrics to a known melody. Take a melody you know: for example, "Alleluia." Instead of singing the words already written, create your own from your heart, singing them to the tune of "Alleluia." You have just painted a heart song!
2. A new melody to known lyrics. Take lyrics you know: for example, "Amazing Grace." Sing those words with a brand new melody. Go up and down in pitch. Create as you go. It's your song!
3. Both a new melody and new lyrics. This is easier when a simple musical underscore is being played (and is most common in a public worship setting). Begin singing a

melody that fits with the underscore being played. Often, one or two notes will work better than others, in terms of not clashing with the instrumental music. Gradually, expand to different notes and melodies. Combined with countless other melodies and countermelodies being sung and played across the congregation, the end result is incredibly dynamic! The entire congregation can experience unity in the ebb and flow, and the crescendo and decrescendo of spontaneous praise and worship!

4. Out-of-the-box methods. While the first three methods lay an important and practical foundation, we would be remiss to confine heart songs to these three approaches. Creativity is encouraged, and expressions that don't fit neatly within the lines of prescribed methods are welcome. We should, of course, keep biblical parameters in mind, but in doing so, we shouldn't be overly restrictive. Let me point out that many evangelical church traditions place importance upon the gifts of the Spirit, and, particularly, the use of a spiritual language. For individuals who operate in such gifts, heart songs can be beautifully expressed as one replaces English words with his or her spiritual language, no longer limited to what the mind can process and articulate, but instead allowing the spirit to express itself with uninterrupted flow. I realize this is a matter of doctrine and may be foreign to those outside of the Pentecostal/Charismatic tradition. Nevertheless, for a greater understanding of the gift of spiritual language, I would recommend *The Beauty of Spiritual Language*, by Dr. Jack Hayford.[38]

Summation

1. The terms "spiritual song," "new song," and "heart song" (*tehillah*) refer to a common concept in scripture, where

[38] Jack W. Hayford, *The Beauty of Spiritual Language* (Nashville, TN: Thomas Nelson, 1996).

individuals release spontaneous songs to the Lord, from their hearts.

2. Though hymns and choruses are essential, heart songs are to be a regular, balanced part of any praise and worship time. Such songs allow individual believers to express themselves through their unique personality and current relationship/walk with the Lord.
3. Heart songs best express our love relationship as children to Daddy God. We paint imperfect yet priceless pictures for our loving Heavenly Father.
4. It is not unspiritual to provide instruction that will develop God's people in bringing forth heart songs.
5. A general understanding of *how* we bring forth heart songs is as follows: The "canvas" is the basic musical underscore. The "paint" is the words of your heart. And the "brush" is the tool (voice or instrument) used to get the paint on the canvas.

Devotional Exercises

1. During personal and corporate times of praise and worship, make an increased effort to experiment with the four types of heart songs listed at the end of this chapter.
2. Play an instrumental CD, open your Bible to the Psalms, and try to sing a heart song. Use scripture as a guide, if you're struggling to come up with words.

Study Guide Questions—Chapter 9

1. If we are instructed in Ephesians and Colossians to praise and worship with psalms, hymns, *and* spiritual songs, why do you suppose the latter is practiced so infrequently in many churches?
2. From your perspective, list the advantages of being able to sing heart songs during times of praise and worship.
3. From your perspective, list the challenges you might experience when trying to sing heart songs.

4. In your current stage of development, if you were to be instructed in the area of singing heart songs, where would you need the most development or training?
5. Of the four types of heart songs described at the end of this chapter, list those in which you have been actively engaged.
6. Briefly relate a memorable experience where you sang heart songs. (If you've never done this, relate a time you perceived others around you flowing in this type of praise and worship.)
7. How will your praise and worship be different as a result of this chapter?

Chapter 10

APPROPRIATING THE POWER OF PRAISE

Part 1

In chapters 8 and 9, we discovered different biblical words for praise, which reinforced the idea that we must not only worship in *spirit*, but also in *truth* (according to the patterns set forth in God's Word).

In *this* chapter, we will discuss three very important biblical principles that will appropriate, or unleash, the full power of our praise. Up to this point in our study, we have learned a lot about praise and worship and have hopefully developed a richer understanding of what it can and should be. We now turn our focus toward making praise and worship more effective. In this chapter and the next, we will begin to see that praise and worship can be a powerful instrument in our hands, to tremendously impact both the spiritual and physical dimensions within which we live and operate on a daily basis.

At this point, let it be said that praise and worship is intended to redeem not only our *relationship* with the living God, but also our *rulership* as kings and priests. Biblical praise and worship should introduce God's kingdom power *to* the church, and extend that power *through* the church. We, as kings and priests, stand between heaven's throne and earth's need. Our offerings of true praise and worship welcome God's rule in man's circumstances.

So for those of us who are serious about making a significant impact, there are three key factors that should be well understood: vocal proclamation, agreement, and moving in unity.

1. The Power of Vocal Proclamation

Read Mark 11:20–24: "In the morning, as they went along, they saw the fig tree withered from the roots. Peter remembered and said to Jesus, 'Rabbi, look! The fig tree you cursed has withered!' 'Have faith in God,' Jesus answered. 'I tell you the truth, if anyone says to this mountain, "Go, throw yourself into the sea," and does not doubt in his heart but believes that what he says will happen, it will be done for him. Therefore I tell you, whatever you ask for in prayer, believe that you have received it, and it will be yours.'"

In the above account, Jesus was teaching His disciples about effective prayer. We see that there was undeniable power in His words to the barren fig tree. His *speaking* caused the tree to wither.

Throughout scripture, great importance is placed upon confession, proclamation, declaration, and vocal affirmation of the truth. Note the following examples to the right: Romans 10:10, Matthew 10:32–33, 1 John 1:9, Romans 10:8.

> Romans 10:10: "For it is with your heart that you believe and are justified, and it is with your mouth that you *confess* and are saved" (emphasis added).
>
> Matthew 10:32–33: "Whoever *acknowledges* me before men, I will also acknowledge him before my Father in heaven. But whoever disowns me before men, I will disown him before my Father in heaven" (emphasis added).
>
> 1 John 1:9: "If we *confess* our sins, he is faithful and just and will forgive us our sins and purify us from all unrighteousness" (emphasis added).
>
> Romans 10:8: "But what does it say? 'The word is near you; it is in your mouth and in your heart,' that is, the word of faith we are *proclaiming*" (emphasis added).

Let's look again at Mark 11:23…

"I tell you the truth, if anyone *says* to this mountain, 'Go, throw yourself into the sea,' and does not doubt in his heart but believes that what he says will happen, it will be done for him" (emphasis added).

Did you catch that? Notice Jesus didn't tell the disciples to whine about the mountain or wish that it be removed. He didn't encourage them to complain about the mountain to their neighbors or establish a committee to deal with it. Rather, He told them to *speak* to it. Now, the scriptures teach a balanced theology concerning this—it's not just about *speaking things forth on a whim*. An abiding relationship with Christ, divine timing, and what's best in light of God's eternal plan are all factors that must be taken into account. Even so, we must not be ignorant of the awesome power of our words! Consider another passage where Jesus is teaching about this…

"But I tell you that men will have to give account on the day of judgment for every careless word they have spoken. For by your words you will be acquitted, and by your words you will be condemned" (Matthew 12:36–37).

There is definitely a difference between *believing* Jesus is your Lord and *declaring* from a believing heart, *"Jesus is my Lord!"* James reminds us that we often have not because we ask not, with believing hearts. Furthermore, he says…

"The tongue also is a fire, a world of evil among the parts of the body. It corrupts the whole person, sets the whole course of his life on fire, and is itself set on fire by hell … With the tongue we praise our Lord and Father, and with it we curse men, who have been made in God's likeness. Out of the same mouth come praise and cursing. My brothers, this should not be" (James 3:6, 9–10).

Above, we see a negative illustration of the tongue's potency. But the tongue is just as powerful when used for righteousness, which is exactly how Paul encourages us to use it…

"I put this in human terms because you are weak in your natural selves. Just as you used to offer the parts of your body in slavery to impurity and to ever-increasing

Psalm 8:2 (KJV): "Out of the mouth of babes and sucklings hast thou ordained *strength* because of thine enemies, that thou mightest still the enemy and the avenger" (emphasis added).

Psalm 8:2 (NIV): "From the lips of children and infants you have ordained *praise* because of your enemies, to silence the foe and the avenger" (emphasis added).

Psalm 149:6–9: "May the praise of God be in their mouths and a double-edged sword in their hands, to inflict vengeance on the nations and punishment on the peoples, to bind their kings with fetters, their nobles with shackles of iron, to carry out the sentence written against them—this is the glory of all his saints. Praise the LORD."

wickedness, so now offer them in slavery to righteousness leading to holiness" (Romans 6:19).

Now consider the power of vocal proclamation in praise and worship. Read Psalm 8:2 and Psalm 149:6–9 on the previous page.

In Psalm 8:2, depending on your translation, you may see the word "strength" or "praise" appear. This is the verse Jesus quoted following the cleansing of the temple and the declaration to all that His Father's house should be a house of prayer (praise, worship, and intercession). Now read the account below…

"'It is written,' he said to them, 'My house will be called a house of prayer, but you are making it a "den of robbers."' The blind and the lame came to him at the temple, and he healed them. But when the chief priests and the teachers of the law saw the wonderful things he did and the children shouting in the temple area, 'Hosanna to the Son of David,' they were indignant. 'Do you hear what these children are saying?' they asked him. 'Yes,' replied Jesus, 'have you never read, "From the lips of children and infants you have ordained *praise*?"'" (Matthew 21:13–16, emphasis added).

The Hebrew word for "strength/praise" used in Psalm 8:2 is Strong's #5797—*oz*—which means "strength in various applications (force, security, majesty, praise, boldness, loud might, power, strength.)"[39] The Greek word used by Jesus in Matthew 21:16 is Strong's *#136—ainos*—which simply means "praise."[40] The two concepts, blended together, depict "strength/praise" that has been given (ordained) because of our enemies and has the power to silence the foe and the avenger! And, even more incredible, this potent weapon of praise can be wielded by the most frail and vulnerable of all—little children and infants! Amazing!

---

[39] *Oz* (Strong's Hb5797) as defined in *A Concise Dictionary of the Words in the Hebrew Bible with Their Renderings in the Authorized English Version* (Nashville, TN: Abingdon Press, 1973), 86.

[40] *Ainos* (Strong's *Gk136*) as defined in *A Concise Dictionary of the Words in the Greek Testament with Their Renderings in the Authorized English Version* (Nashville, TN: Abingdon Press, 1973), 8.

Let's further discover the power of vocal proclamations of praise as we again read Psalm 149:6–9…

"May the praise of God be in their mouths and a double-edged sword in their hands, to inflict vengeance on the nations and punishment on the peoples, to bind their kings with fetters, their nobles with shackles of iron, to carry out the sentence written against them. This is the glory of all his saints. Praise the LORD."

"Praise" in verse 6 is the Hebrew word *rowmemah*.[41] This type of praise is in their mouths and the sword is in their hands—*to* or *for the purpose of:*

- Inflicting vengeance on nations
- Inflicting punishment on peoples
- Binding kings with fetters
- Binding nobles with shackles of iron
- And carrying out the sentence written against them

Psalm 144:1–2: "Praise be to the Lord, my Rock, who trains my hands for war, my fingers for battle. He is my loving God and my fortress, my stronghold and my deliverer, my shield, in whom I take refuge, who subdues peoples under me."

(See an additional reference, Psalm 144:1–2, to the left.)

Please remember, as New Testament believers, we have learned that physical shadows in the Old Testament (i.e., the tabernacle of Moses) are often spiritual realities in the New Testament (i.e., the heavenly throne room). We are also told point-blank by the apostle Paul in Ephesians 6:12 that our struggle is *not* against flesh and blood (physical nations, peoples, kings, and nobles), but against spiritual rulers, authorities, powers of the dark world, and forces of evil in the heavenly realms!

Here's the point. As singers declare the greatness of God, and musicians add agreement on their instruments, the resulting praise ascends into the heavenly realms and actually wars on their behalf.

---

41 *Rowmamah* (Strong's Hb7319) as defined in *A Concise Dictionary of the Words in the Hebrew Bible with Their Renderings in the Authorized English Version* (Nashville, TN: Abingdon Press, 1973), 107.

Word-enriched vocal proclamations of high praise bind spiritual strongmen (kings) and their demonic assistants (nobles) with fetters and shackles, inflict vengeance and punishment on demonic hordes (nations and peoples), and carry out the sentence written against them. What is that sentence, you might ask? Note the scriptures to the right (Hebrews 2:14, 1 John 3:8, Ephesians 1:19–22, Colossians 2:15).

The glory of the saints, according to Psalm 149:9, is to speak Word-enriched high praise to bind up illegal powers and carry out the sentence of powerlessness against them, which Jesus secured through His death and resurrection.

Our enemies' sentence was written over two thousand years ago. Their legal reign was destroyed. Their authority was disarmed. They were rendered *powerless*!

> Hebrews 2:14: "Since the children have flesh and blood, he too shared in their humanity so that by his death he might *destroy him who holds the power of death*—that is, the devil" (emphasis added).
>
> 1 John 3:8: "The reason the Son of God appeared was to *destroy the devil's work*" (emphasis added).
>
> Ephesians 1:19–22: "That power is like the working of his mighty strength, which he exerted in Christ when he raised him from the dead and seated him at his right hand in the heavenly realms, far above all rule and authority, power and dominion, and every title that can be given, not only in the present age but also in the one to come. And God *placed all things under his feet* and appointed him to be head over everything for the church" (emphasis added).
>
> Colossians 2:15: "And having *disarmed the powers and authorities*, he made a public spectacle of them, triumphing over them by the cross" (emphasis added).

What Does This Mean?

Just as there's a difference between *believing* Jesus is your Lord and *declaring* from a believing heart, "*Jesus is my Lord,*" there's also a difference between halfheartedly singing, "No weapon formed against me will prosper" and boldly declaring, with full faith and understanding, "No weapon formed against me will prosper!" *Your faith-filled declaration actually makes a difference in the spiritual realm!*

- Feelings of despair and discouragement can actually be altered by declaring in song, *"On Christ, the Solid Rock, I stand!"*
- Enemy oppression can actually be broken by declaring, *"The enemy has been defeated, and death couldn't hold You down!"*

- Defeat brought on by the powers of darkness can actually be turned by declaring, *"In the name of Jesus, we have the victory!"*
- Spiritual strength, help, and protection can actually be released from heaven's storehouse as faith-filled lips declare, *"You are my shield, my strength, my portion, deliverer, my shelter, strong tower, my very present help in time of need!"*

2. The Power of Agreement

Agreement is the second key factor in making our praise and worship powerful and effective. The need for agreement among believers is seen throughout scripture…

"Do two walk together unless they have agreed to do so?" (Amos 3:3).

"I appeal to you, brothers, in the name of our Lord Jesus Christ, that all of you agree with one another so that there may be no divisions among you and that you may be perfectly united in mind and thought" (1 Corinthians 1:10).

Note below the importance Jesus placed on agreement in seeking answers to prayer…

"Again, I tell you that if two of you on earth agree about anything you ask for, it will be done for you by my Father in heaven" (Matthew 18:19).

The Ministry of Amen

Agreement is precisely why we say "amen" during church services. We don't do it to encourage the preacher (although it can encourage him or her). We do it because of Jesus's words that *if two agree, it shall be done!* Let me explain.

When a preacher, teacher, or any believer declares:

- "God is going to pour out His Spirit in this place like never before" or
- "God is raising this church up to make a significant impact in our city"

And... an individual or group says "amen," a.k.a., "so be it," something significant happens. Things in the spiritual realm are set into motion that actually bring that statement closer to fruition than before the "amen" was added.

It's a concept people have been familiar with for years. It's called *synergy*, and it's defined in Webster's as "the increased effectiveness that results when two or more people work together"[42]—a.k.a., in agreement. Said another way, synergy causes people to realize more *together* than they could ever realize *individually*. The creation of a whole is greater than the sum of its parts; in other words, 2 + 2 = 5, when synergy comes into play.

How This Applies to Praise and Worship

Simply put, we were not meant to function as spiritual lone rangers. We need each other. This is why Paul stated that one part of the body shouldn't say to the other, "I have no need of you." Similarly, the writer to the Hebrews declared, "Let us not give up meeting together as some are in the habit of doing."

Yes, gathering together corporately is important. And, in those corporate settings, if you are seeking the Lord for an answer to a specific prayer request, it is helpful to seek others out who will agree with you concerning the request. This is not just a way of providing fellowship and support, nor does it devalue individual prayers; rather, there is something that happens in the spiritual realm when there is that added dimension of agreement.

Now I believe what's true for prayer is also true for praise and worship. In fact, praise and worship is a *form* of prayer, as we've already pointed out. It is communication with God. So, while individuals can and should praise and worship daily on their own, there is something unique that happens when several believers gather for times of praise and worship. And I believe there is extraordinary power released when those believers truly come together in agreement!

---

42 Synergy—a simple definition, as appearing in *Merriam-Webster Dictionary*, 2016 edition.

For example, it is wonderful for you to sing songs such as "Create in Me a Clean Heart, O God" in your personal worship time. But when you sing this alongside your brothers and sisters, there is the added dimension of agreement, and Jesus said if two or more agree, it shall be done! This is not to say that agreement alone produces the clean heart. We still must submit our will to his cleansing, but the added agreement does *synergize* the prayer request.

When together we sing "Nothing is impossible for you," is this not a powerful prayer of agreement? So many of our praise and worship songs are really powerful prayers. Let's sing them with faith and understanding, together, in agreement. As we do, I believe we will begin to see praise and worship become powerfully effective in our lives and circumstances!

3. The Power of Moving in Unity

Moving in unity is the third key factor in making our praise and worship powerful and effective. Closely related to agreement, moving in unity takes steps beyond simply agreeing, so we're actually moving forward together. It's one thing to get people to agree; it's quite another to get them to function "as one man." Yet, throughout scripture, and in every revival of church history, powerful things happened when groups of believers moved in unity. Interestingly, more times than not, the catalyst for a powerful intervention from God was not just unity but *unity in praise and worship!*

Let's note some scriptural examples.

Below, you will see a negative instance of moving together in unity…

The Tower of Babel (Genesis 11:6):

"The LORD said, 'If as one people speaking the same language they have begun to do this, then nothing they plan to do will be impossible for them.'"

Here, due to the power of unity, God saw a need to intervene because the people were moving together, but in the *wrong direction.*

How much more will moving in unity be blessed of God when His people head in the *right direction*? Let's see…

The wall of Jericho on the edge of the Promised Land (Joshua 6:2–3, 5):

"The Lord said to Joshua, 'See, I have delivered Jericho into your hands … march around the city … when you hear them sound a long blast on the trumpets, have *all the people* give a loud shout'" (emphasis added). They did, and the walls fell down!

The successful return of the Ark to Israel (2 Samuel 6:15):

"*The entire house* of Israel brought up the Ark of the Lord with shouts and the sound of trumpets" (emphasis added).

The installation of the Ark in Solomon's Temple and the coming of God's glory (2 Chronicles 5:13–14):

"The trumpeters and singers joined in unison, *as with one voice*, to give praise and thanks to the Lord. Accompanied by trumpets, cymbals and other instruments, they raised their voices in praise to the Lord and sang: 'he is good, his love endures forever.' Then, the temple of the Lord was filled with a cloud, and the priests could not perform their service because of the cloud. For the glory of the Lord filled the temple of God" (emphasis added).

The rebuilding of the altar and temple foundation under Ezra (Ezra 3:1, 2, 10–11):

"When the seventh month came and the Israelites had settled in their towns, the people assembled *as one man* in Jerusalem … and [they] began to build the altar of the God of Israel … when the builders laid the foundation of the temple … with praise and thanksgiving they sang to the Lord … and *all the people* gave a great shout of praise to the Lord" (emphasis added).

The completion of the walls under Nehemiah (Nehemiah 8:1, 3, 5–6):

"*All the people* assembled *as one man* in the square before the Water Gate. They told Ezra the scribe to bring out the Book of the Law of Moses, which the Lord had commanded for Israel ... He read it aloud from daybreak till noon ... and *all the people* listened attentively to the Book of the Law ... The people could see him because he was standing above them; and as he opened it, *all the people* stood up. Ezra praised the Lord, the great God; and *all the people* lifted their hands and responded, 'Amen! Amen!' Then they bowed down and worshiped the Lord with their faces to the ground" (emphasis added).

Jesus's final prayer for all believers before his arrest, sentence, and crucifixion (John 17:20–21):

"I pray ... that *all of them* may be *one*, Father, just as you are in me and I am in you. May they also be in us so that the world may believe that you have sent me" (emphasis added).

The Holy Spirit's outpouring at Pentecost (Acts 2, 4):

"When the day of Pentecost came, they were *all together* in one place ... (c2, v44) ... and *all the believers* were together and had everything in common ... (c4, v32) ... *all the believers* were *one* in heart and mind" (emphasis added).

Clearly, if we are serious about gaining significant ground against our enemy—if we desire to move aggressively forward in our relationship with God, we must embrace the fact that moving in unity "as one man" is a key, especially during times of praise and worship. I would propose that there is far too much individualized praise and worship in corporate settings. When we gather together, we need to accomplish something together, not just "do our own thing." Let's not offer individual offerings, as those who happen to be standing in the same room but are heading in entirely different directions. Let's lift up praise and worship together, in unity, and watch what God does!

I'm absolutely confident of this. When we, as God's people, rise up as a mighty army and begin to actually move forward in unity, declaring the high praises of God in the face of the enemy and every circumstance contrary to God's will, we will begin to see the plans of the wicked frustrated and God's purposes furthered in our lives and churches!

Summation

1. Praise and worship can be a powerful instrument, impacting both the spiritual and physical dimensions within which we live and operate on a daily basis.
2. There is an added dimension of power as belief in the heart is vocalized, or declared aloud.
3. Agreement of two of more believers produces power in prayer. In the same way, as two or more sing psalms, hymns, and spiritual songs during corporate times of praise and worship, synergy comes into play, and extraordinary power is released.
4. A group of believers moving together "as one man" is extremely powerful. Such unity has been the catalyst for divine intervention, in biblical times and throughout church history.

Devotional Exercises

1. Think of some of your favorite songs—hymns or choruses. What truths are being declared or proclaimed as these songs are sung?
2. Begin spending time in prayer for your congregation—that the people will commit to vocal proclamation, agreement, and moving forward in unity during corporate praise and worship times.

Study Guide Questions—Chapter 10

1. Considering what you have learned about the power of vocal proclamation, how might this truth affect *your* praise and worship?
2. Reread Psalm 149:6–9. List some spiritual kings or nobles or mountains of spiritual resistance in your life. Take a few moments to lift up high praises, binding these principalities of darkness.

3. In your own words, explain why agreement is important in praise and worship, according to Matthew 18:19.
4. Describe a time in which a corporate prayer (two or more agreeing) produced a speedy or powerful answer from on high.
5. If the congregation would choose to truly operate "as one man," what do you think might happen?
6. Read the entire story of the fall of Jericho (Joshua 6). Then answer the following.
    a) In what ways do you think the people might have been tempted to rebel against Joshua's instructions?
    b) How would disunity have impacted the results?
7. When a pastor, worship leader, or individual flowing in spiritual gifts encourages the congregation toward a particular action, what barriers might cause people to resist a unified response?
8. What was the most important thing you learned in this chapter?

Chapter 11

APPROPRIATING THE POWER OF PRAISE

Part 2

In chapter 10, we discovered three key factors that will appropriate or unleash the power of praise: vocal proclamation, agreement, and moving in unity. This chapter, though similar in content, will focus on the *results* of appropriating that power.

1. Praise silences the foe and the avenger.

Remember Psalm 8:2: "From the lips of children and infants you have ordained praise because of your enemies, to silence the foe and the avenger."

In other words, *praise silences the enemy.* Remember, we're not wrestling against flesh and blood, but spiritual powers and principalities that constantly war against the people of God. And the battlefield is most often in the mind.

A. Praise defeats the voice of the enemy *internally* by:
Silencing the voice of temptation.

The enemy may come to us in our minds and begin to tempt us by placing wrong thoughts there. Those thoughts, if not addressed, will begin to squeeze in and overwhelm us. But as we begin to praise God, the thoughts are silenced because we can't concentrate on them and the Lord at the same time. By an act of our will, then, we must turn away from the voices of temptation and actively begin to praise God. The net effect is that our praising over time actually causes those voices of temptation to grow strangely dim, and we eventually don't give them any credence. Let's get our focus where it should be instead of falling into the trap outlined in James chapter 1…

"But each one is tempted when, by his own evil desire, he is dragged away and enticed. Then, after desire has conceived, it gives birth to sin; and sin, when it is full-grown, gives birth to death." (James 1:14-15).

Persistent praise short-circuits this process. It stops the enemy in his tracks!

Silencing the voice of despair.

In a similar way, the enemy will try to cause our thought patterns to head into a downward spiral. This begins with *discouragement*, which leads to *depression*, which leads to *despair*, where we actually feel utter hopelessness. This doesn't just happen overnight, but it's a process that occurs over time, eventually forming a stronghold, as we continue to feed on the lies of the enemy. The negative voices begin to take up residence in our minds. *But* praise shifts our focus away from problems, toward God's awesome ability; away from imperfections, toward God's matchless character; and away from the enemy's lies, toward God's unchanging truth!

David discovered this powerful truth about praise. Read the excerpt from Psalm 42 below. In verses 9–10, David is caught in a downward spiral. Then in verse 11, he actually turns to God in praise, and the voice of despair is silenced…

"I say to God my Rock, 'Why have you forgotten me? Why must I go about mourning, oppressed by the enemy?' My bones suffer mortal agony as my foes taunt me, saying to me all day long, 'Where is your God?' Why are you downcast, O my soul? Why so disturbed within me? Put your hope in God, for I will yet praise him, my Savior and my God" (Psalm 42:9–11).

It's as if you can hear him saying, "If God be for me, who can be against me? I *will* be successful!" (not positive thinking alone, but *belief in the truth*). Let's read on…

"Vindicate me, O God, and plead my cause against an ungodly nation; rescue me from deceitful and wicked men. You are God my stronghold. Why have you rejected me? Why must I go about mourning, oppressed by the enemy? Send forth your light and your truth, let them guide me; let them bring me to your holy mountain, to the place where you dwell. Then I will go to the altar of God, to God, my joy and my delight. I will praise you with the harp, O God, my God. Why are you downcast, O my soul? Why so disturbed within me? Put your hope in God, for I will yet praise him, my Savior and my God" (Psalm 43).

Clearly, through praise and worship, we become consumed with the fullness of God's ability, the nature of His character, and the power of His truth, rather than being consumed with lies and "defeatist-type" attitudes of gloom, dread, discouragement, depression, and despair—all of the things the devil tries to establish in our minds. Praise has the power to get us back on track! Consider the words of the apostle Paul…

"Finally, brothers, whatever is true, whatever is noble, whatever is right, whatever is pure, whatever is lovely, whatever is admirable—if anything is excellent or praiseworthy—think about such things. Whatever you have learned or received or heard from me, or seen in me—put it into practice. And the God of peace will be with you" (Philippians 4:8–9).

Praise short-circuits the processes of sin and despair in our minds, which the enemy initiates and attempts to feed.

And praise not only silences the enemy *internally*, but *externally* as well.

B. Praise silences the foe and avenger *outwardly* by giving the enemy indisputable evidence of his defeat.

When we begin to praise God, we proclaim His ability, His truth, and all that He is in the face of our attacker. Our praise confronts the enemy, intimidates him, and causes him to shut his lying mouth! The enemy's voice is silenced!

In essence, it's what '80s/'90s Christian singer and songwriter Carman used to say: "When the devil reminds you of your past, you remind him of his future!" As we confront the enemy with praise, we actually look him in the eye and declare the greatness and wonder of God, who has already defeated him on our behalf. We declare, with a heart of faith, our allegiance to the truth instead of the devil's lies.

One of my favorite passages of scripture is 2 Chronicles 20, where vocal praise becomes a weapon of war that outwardly defeats the enemy. See the condensed passage below…

> The Spirit of the Lord came on Jahaziel … a Levite and descendant of Asaph, as he stood in the assembly. He said: "Listen, King Jehoshaphat and all who live in Judah and Jerusalem! This is what the Lord says to you: 'Do not be afraid or discouraged because of this vast army. For the battle is not yours, but God's. Tomorrow march down against them. They will be climbing up by the Pass of Ziz, and you will find them at the end of the gorge in the Desert of Jeruel. You will not have to fight this battle. Take up your positions; stand firm and see the deliverance the Lord will give you, O Judah and Jerusalem. Do not be afraid; do not be discouraged. Go out to face them tomorrow, and the Lord will be with you.'" Jehoshaphat bowed with his face to the ground, and all the people of Judah and Jerusalem fell down in worship before the Lord. Then some Levites from the Kohathites and Korahites stood up and praised the Lord, the God of Israel, with a very loud voice. Early

> in the morning they left for the Desert of Tekoa. As they set out, Jehoshaphat stood and said, "Listen to me, Judah and people of Jerusalem! Have faith in the Lord your God and you will be upheld; have faith in his prophets and you will be successful." After consulting the people, Jehoshaphat appointed men to sing to the Lord and to praise him for the splendor of his holiness as they went out at the head of the army, saying: "Give thanks to the Lord, for his love endures forever" (2 Chronicles 20:14-21).

As King Jehoshaphat and the Israelites humbled themselves before God—and as singers and musicians praised Jehovah at the front lines of battle against the enemy—the Lord set ambushes, and enemy nations actually destroyed one another. As was promised, the battle was not the Israelites', but rather, God's. He fought for them as they put their trust in Him and praised Him wholeheartedly. Amazing!

So we see the power of praise to silence the foe and the avenger both inwardly *and* outwardly, as the enemy is directly confronted. But there's something else here.

2. Praise brings strength to the believer.

We've all heard that the joy of the Lord is our strength. True. But *praise* also brings strength to the believer, while at the same time silencing the foe and the avenger; it's a double-edged sword. Remember again this truth from our last chapter…

"From the lips of children and infants you have ordained *praise*" (Psalm 8:2a, emphasis added).

The King James Version actually says "strength" instead of "praise" (Heb. *oz*). Harris, Archer, and Waltke say the following in the *Theological Wordbook of the Old Testament* concerning this word:

"Not only is strength a quality given by God; He himself is that strength. In seeking (His) presence, then, strength is found. The impartation of His strength made the psalmist secure as a strong mountain. Thus, in hymns of praise, God's strength appears."[43]

In other words, as we begin to praise in this way, strength is actually imparted to us. *Praise produces strength.* Furthermore, remember who is vocalizing this strength/praise in Psalm 8:2—children and infants (or babes and sucklings in the KJV). Other versions speak of nursing infants, which is really intriguing.

Psalm 8:2 and Matthew 21:16 (Jesus's quotation of Psalm 8:2) both depict the weakest, most vulnerable individual from which strength is ordained. Realize, we're not talking about kings or princes. The scripture doesn't say, "Out of the mouths of kings and princes and other mighty men of valor, God has ordained strength/praise." No. Strength/praise is ordained from the mouths of the weakest, most dependent people! The apostle Paul affirms…

"But God chose the foolish things of the world to shame the wise; God chose the weak things of the world to shame the strong. He chose the lowly things of this world and the despised things—and the things that are not—to nullify the things that are, so that no one may boast before him" (1 Corinthians 1:27–29).

No matter how weak you are, no matter how powerless you feel, no matter how vulnerable you become in any situation—as you begin to praise God, as you begin to declare the truth in song, *God's supernatural strength begins to take up residency within you!* You begin to face the situation, not in your own limitation, but with the sufficiency and power of God, that He might receive glory. Praise is your means of recovery and restoration!

No wonder praise is such an integral part of any church service. It prepares us to receive a Word from God and fully submit to His Spirit, so our hearts and minds are strengthened and renewed.

Not only does praise silence the voice of the enemy and bring strength, but:

---

[43] C. Shultz, "*oz*," in *Theological Wordbook of the Old Testament*, edited by R. Laird Harris, Gleason L. Archer Jr., and Bruce K. Waltke (Chicago, IL: Moody, 1980), 2:659–60.

3. **Praise shatters evil restraints and opens the door of God's will for our lives.**

Consider the account of Paul and Silas in prison, recorded in Acts 16. If you remember the story, they were going to the place of prayer. Along the way, they met a slave girl who had a spirit whereby she could predict the future. When they cast the evil spirit out of her, the girl's owners realized that their hopes of making money were gone. They became angry and brought Paul and Silas before the authorities. They claimed that these Christian men were throwing the city into an uproar, and the crowd was incited against them. Subsequently, Paul and Silas were stripped, flogged, and thrown into prison. The jailer was ordered to guard them carefully. Let's read the end of the account…

"Upon receiving such orders, he put them in the inner cell and fastened their feet in the stocks. About midnight Paul and Silas were praying and singing hymns to God, and the other prisoners were listening to them. Suddenly there was such a violent earthquake that the foundations of the prison were shaken. At once all the prison doors flew open, and everybody's chains came loose" (Acts 16:24–26).

At this, the jailer awakened and was going to kill himself. Paul shouted, "No, don't harm yourself; we are all here!" Then the jailer asked, "What must I do to be saved?" and Paul and Silas led him to the Lord, he and his entire household. As you consider the unfolding of the account, note the following points that can, in turn, be applied to our lives.

A. "It was about midnight…"

They had been stripped, badly beaten, and thrown into the inner cell. They were now under guard. Yet, in the middle of the night, with darkness all around, in the midst of that hellish environment, they made a choice to lift their voices and sing praise to God. (They didn't even have an instrument or lyrics on a screen.) And there, in that dark, dank cellar, God began to undertake!

In the lives of many people—maybe you—it's midnight. Things look dark. Things seem hopeless. It's a scary place to be, but take courage. God has not forgotten you. He has not forsaken you. He has not left you to rot with the rats in the cellar. In the midst of your trial, in the midst of your pain, in the midst of your hurt, as you look at circumstances and feel that your hands are tied, don't be discouraged. Don't be fearful. God has not called you to this prison cell. His purpose for your life extends beyond the darkness of a dungeon. Therefore, in the midst of your midnight, as an act of your will, lift up your voice and sing praise to God, so others in prison around you who find themselves stuck in similar hopeless circumstances will hear you and find encouragement. And God will begin to undertake!

B. "There came a great earthquake..."

We often look entirely at the physical, but as we've already stated, our struggle is spiritual, not of the flesh. We do not wage war as the world does. Our weapons are not carnal (worldly). Rather, they are mighty for pulling down spiritual strongholds. You may not see anything happening in the physical, but remember that Jesus said, "Stop judging by outward appearances only." We may not feel physical earthquakes shaking our feet as we praise God. But I believe, as we begin to lift our voices and offer up faith-filled praise, there is a shockwave sent through the foundations of the spiritual realm. The ground begins to tremble under the feet of powers and principalities of darkness. They begin to lose their footing. They begin to be caught off balance, and the effects are realized in the earth and in our tangible circumstances!

C. "The chains were unfastened..."

The physical restraints that the enemy used to impede and restrict these men of God came loose and fell to the ground. What are those things the enemy has bound you up with? Fear? Past? Complacency? Sin? How has he tried to tie you up—to prevent you from doing God's will and become your very best for the Lord? As you praise God, I believe those restraints can be loosed and dismantled.

Realize that this wasn't the end of the story for Paul and Silas—and it's not the end of the story for *you*! They still had to go to

Thessalonica. Paul still had to stand in the arena at Athens and proclaim that Jesus Christ was the "Unknown God." He still needed to disciple new converts in Corinth and Ephesus. God still had a plan for Paul and Silas to fulfill. He wasn't done with them, so the Lord made a way. Their deliverance was at hand!

D. "The doors of the prison were opened!"

Let me say it this way: Paul and Silas were being hindered from going forward in God's will. But their praise in the night season opened the door for His will to be fulfilled. In the same way, as we look at our lives, there are things very real and tangible that the enemy has used to incarcerate us. Doors are locked and shut—doors that keep us from moving forward in God's plans and purposes. It's like we have been placed under guard, in an inner cell. But listen, a people free to praise God cannot be imprisoned long by demonic forces. The prison doors are coming open!

Make no mistake about it—in the midst of your darkest hour, as you lift up your voice, affirm your faith, and boldly declare the praises of Him who has called you, not only will the foundations of hell begin to shake and shudder—not only will the strategies of the evil one begin to crumble—not only will the chains begin to fall off—but prison doors that have been locked for years, barriers that have impeded and impaired the will of God for your life, will begin to rattle. Locks will shake loose, and to the amazement of those around you, the doors will swing wide open, allowing God's will to move forward in your life!

As we conclude this lesson, I want to point out that the jailer and his entire household were saved, as a result of this God encounter. Not only were Paul and Silas miraculously delivered, but lost people turned to the Lord as well. I would suggest that this is evangelistic worship in its truest sense—people being drawn into an experience with God who do not

> 1 Corinthians 14:24–25: "But if an unbeliever or someone who does not understand comes in while everybody is prophesying, he will be convinced by all that he is a sinner and will be judged by all, and the secrets of his heart will be laid bare. So he will fall down and worship God, exclaiming, 'God is really among you!'"

know Him, as a result of His work among His people. Could it be that we have made evangelistic worship too palatable and nonthreatening to the unbeliever, in an effort to avoid offending him or her? It seems that the early church was experiencing the power of God in such a way that unbelievers would come into a meeting, fall on their faces, and state that God was truly present. (See 1 Corinthians 14:24–25). May we cultivate those kinds of encounters today, so that God may be glorified and hearts may be changed!

Summation

1. Praise silences the voices of temptation and despair in the battlefield of our minds.
2. Praise silences the enemy by giving him indisputable evidence of his defeat.
3. Praise produces strength in the worshiper.
4. Praise shakes the foundations of hell, shatters evil restraints, and opens doors for God's will to be done in our lives.

Devotional Exercise

The next time you are tempted or discouraged with certain thoughts in your mind, stop what you are doing and begin to praise God, proclaiming His ability and exalting His character. Note what happens as a result.

Study Guide Questions—Chapter 11

1. In your own words, explain how shifting the focus from our problems to God's ability and character transforms our circumstances.
2. Explain how praise intimidates the enemy.
3. How might praise produce strength in the worshiper?
4. Give some thought to the story of Paul and Silas in prison—how the situation applies to *your* life and circumstances.
    a) What "evil restraints" are in your life?
    b) What "closed doors" keep you from moving forward with what you perceive as God's will for your life?

5. If you were in Paul and Silas's circumstances, what would be the hardest thing for you to overcome, in order to do what they did?
6. How has the Holy Spirit applied this chapter to your life, and how will you be changed as a result?

SET LIST EXERCISES

Directions:

1. For each set list provided, describe the interaction taking place between God and the worshiper.
2. Chart the progression, from the outer court, through the holy place, and into the holy of holies.
3. List biblical references and/or scriptural principles found in each song.
4. Indicate which Hebrew expression(s) of "praise" would be most appropriate for each song.
5. In one sentence, state the primary theme of this worship service.

(Use a separate sheet of paper if necessary.)

Worship service
May 17, 2015

"Glorious"
"This Is Amazing Grace"
"Forever (We Sing Hallelujah)"
"How Great Thou Art"
"Great Are You, Lord"

"Glorious"
My God, You reign forever and ever, how great Your name
Your love remains forever and ever, You stay the same
Shout it out, shout it out if you know He's good
Sing it out, sing it out, for the Lord is good
Shout it out loud, "You are glorious"
Glorious, shout it out and
Glorious, make it loud and
Jesus, we shout Your name, Jesus, we make Your praise
Glorious, You are glorious
Shine, Jesus, You shine for all the world to see
You are glorious

Copyright 2012 Integrity's Praise! Music, Sound of the New Breed, DLD Music, Centricity Songs, and R E M Publishing

"This Is Amazing Grace"

Who breaks the power of sin and darkness?
Whose love is mighty and so much stronger?
The King of Glory, the King above all kings
Who shakes the whole earth with holy thunder?
Who leaves us breathless in awe and wonder?
The King of Glory, the King above all kings
This is amazing grace, this is unfailing love
That You would take my place, that You would bear my cross
You laid down Your life that I would be set free
Oh, Jesus I sing for all that You've done for me
Worthy is the Lamb Who was slain
Worthy is the King Who conquered the grave
Worthy is the Lamb Who was slain, worthy, worthy, worthy

Copyright 2012 Phil Wickham Music, Seems Like Music, Sing My Songs, W.B. Music Corp., and Bethel Music Publishing

"Forever (We Sing Hallelujah)"

The moon and stars, they wept, the morning sun was dead
The Savior of the world was fallen
His body on the cross, His blood poured out for us
The weight of every curse upon Him
One final breath He gave as heaven looked away
The Son of God was laid in darkness
A battle in the grave, the war on death was waged
The pow'r of hell forever broken
The ground began to shake, the stone was rolled away
His perfect love could not be overcome
Now death, where is your sting?
Our resurrected King has rendered you defeated
Forever He is glorified, forever He is lifted high
Forever He is risen, He is alive, He is alive
We sing hallelujah, we sing hallelujah
We sing hallelujah, the Lamb has overcome

Copyright 2013 KAJE Songs, Worship Together Music, and Bethel Music Publishing

"How Great Thou Art"
Oh Lord, my God, when I in awesome wonder
Consider all the worlds Thy hands have made
I see the stars, I hear the rolling thunder
Thy pow'r throughout the universe displayed
Then sings my soul, my Savior God to Thee
How great Thou art, how great Thou art

Copyright 1953 Stuart K. Hine Trust

"Great Are You, Lord"
You give life, You are love, You bring light to the darkness
You give hope, You restore ev'ry heart that is broken
Great are You, Lord
It's Your breath in our lungs, so we pour out our praise
Pour out our praise
It's Your breath in our lungs, so we pour out our praise to You only
All the earth will shout Your praise
Our hearts will cry, these bones will sing, "Great are You, Lord"

Copyright 2012 Integrity Music Publishing, Open Hands Music, and So Essential Tunes

Worship service
July 13, 2008

"Say So"
"You Are Good"
"From the Inside Out"
"Surrender"
"At Your Cross (Facedown)"

"Say So"
What does it mean to be saved, isn't it more than just a prayer to pray
More than just a way to heaven?
What does it mean to be His, to be formed in His likeness
Know that we have a purpose?
To be salt and light in the world, in the world
To be salt and light in the world

Let the redeemed of the Lord say so
Let the redeemed of the Lord say so
Let the redeemed of the Lord say so, say so, say so
I am redeemed, I am redeemed, I am redeemed, I am redeemed
I am redeemed, I am redeemed

Copyright 2006 Integrity Music Publishing, New Breed Extended, and Sound of the New Breed

"You Are Good"

Lord, You are good, and Your mercy endureth forever
Lord, You are good, and Your mercy endureth forever
People from every nation and tongue
From generation to generation
We worship You! Hallelujah, hallelujah!
We worship You for Who You are
We worship You! Hallelujah, hallelujah!
We worship You for Who You are, and You are good
Yes You are! Yes You are! Yes You are! So good! So good!
Yes You are! Yes You are! Yes You are!
You are good all the time! All the time You are good!
You are good all the time! All the time You are good!

Copyright 2001 Integrity's Praise! Music and Sound of the New Breed

"From the Inside Out"

A thousand times I've failed, still Your mercy remains
And should I stumble again, still I'm caught in Your grace
Everlasting, Your light will shine when all else fades
Never-ending, Your glory goes beyond all fame
My heart and my soul, I give You control
Consume me from the inside out Lord
Let justice and praise become my embrace
To love You from the inside out
Everlasting, Your light will shine when all else fades
Never-ending, Your glory goes beyond all fame
And the cry of my heart is to bring You praise
From the inside out, Lord, my soul cries out

Copyright 2005 Hillsong Music Publishing

"Surrender"
I'm giving You my heart and all that is within
I lay it all down for the sake of You, my King
I'm giving You my dreams, I'm laying down my rights
I'm giving up my pride for the promise of new life
And I surrender all to You, all to You
And I surrender all to You, all to You

Copyright 2000 Vineyard Music UK

"At Your Cross (Facedown)"
At Your cross, I fall facedown, at Your feet, I lay myself
Holding nothing back here in this time with You, with You
If my lungs can't sing, I'll sing with my heart, with my soul
With my mind, yeah, I'll sing it for You
I fall facedown to show my love
I fall facedown, Lord, make me new again

Copyright 2008 Integrity's Praise! Music

Chapter 12

WORSHIPING IN THE WOMB OF SUFFERING (DEVELOPING DEPTH AND CHARACTER IN WORSHIP)

We come now to the final chapter in our study of praise and worship, but the beginning of the rest of our journey. I am sure you've learned to appreciate and enjoy praise and worship, but the focus of this lesson is somewhat different. In the paragraphs that follow, we want to prepare you for continued growth in your living interaction with God and true depth in your worship life.

Praise and worship can very easily become surface excitement. It needs to be much more, though. It needs to be a lifestyle that sustains us in all circumstances, built upon the unchanging ability and character of God, not upon our shifting circumstances or emotions.

Are you serious about your growth in the Lord? Do you truly want to be more like Jesus—to know Him better? Then you must be willing to go with Him into the garden—into the womb of suffering—where parts of you will die and attitudes will be re-formed. This is where behaviors are retooled and character is forged. It is from this "womb of suffering" that you will emerge more Christ-like and established in your faith, but not without tears and battle scars. Jeremiah describes this experience as being on the potter's

> Jeremiah 18:1–6: "This is the word that came to Jeremiah from the Lord: 'Go down to the potter's house, and there I will give you my message.' So I went down to the potter's house, and I saw him working at the wheel. But the pot he was shaping from the clay was marred in his hands; so the potter formed it into another pot, shaping it as seemed best to him. Then the word of the Lord came to me: 'O house of Israel, can I not do with you as this potter does?' declares the Lord. 'Like clay in the hand of the potter, so are you in my hand, O house of Israel.'"

wheel (Jeremiah 18). The hands of the Master remold our appearance and remake our purpose.

We do not rejoice in the pain of the process, but we can and should rejoice over the process itself. This is why James said…

"Consider it pure joy, my brothers, whenever you face trials of many kinds, because you know that the testing of your faith develops perseverance. Perseverance must finish its work so that you may be mature and complete, not lacking anything" (James 1:2-4).

The joy comes not from the pain, but from knowing that the process is building depth of character in us!

The Old Testament provides numerous examples of people in the womb of suffering, who chose to worship God in the midst of their pain. Perhaps none is more familiar than the instance where Abraham was called upon to sacrifice his only son, Isaac, to God…

"Take your son, your only son, Isaac, whom you love, and go to the region of Moriah. Sacrifice him there as a burnt offering on one of the mountains I will tell you about" (Genesis 22:2).

What God was asking must have seemed totally contrary to His very nature! Abraham's mind was probably reeling as he saddled his donkey for the journey, with thoughts such as, "Why, God? Did You not promise this son to me? Will You now take my joy?"

But the heart matured through years of worship eased the mind tormented by one day's turmoil. Abraham knew what kind of God he served; so he obeyed the Lord, notwithstanding the frightening vision of his only son being sacrificed on a pile of wood! Abraham built an altar, placed wood on it, bound his son, Isaac, laid him upon the wood, and stretched out his hand to slay the boy. But an angel of the Lord interrupted…

"'Do not lay a hand on the boy,' he [the angel] said. 'Do not do anything to him. Now I know that you fear God, because you have not withheld from me your son, your only son.'" (Genesis 22:12).

At that point, thc Lord provided another sacrifice, a ram caught by its horns in a thicket. Abraham gladly offered the sacrificial ram, and father and son worshiped together on that mountain. Abraham had answered the call to worship in that difficult moment, and, at a place called Moriah, God had met him.

Consider the fact that Abraham modeled faith and obedience that's highly unparalleled in today's church, and we shouldn't overlook his simple willingness to worship in the midst of suffering.

Let's continue our study, reading the following passage from Hebrews chapter 12...

> Therefore, since we are surrounded by such a great cloud of witnesses, let us throw off everything that hinders and the sin that so easily entangles, and let us run with perseverance the race marked out for us. Let us fix our eyes on Jesus, the author and perfecter of our faith, who for the joy set before him endured the cross, scorning its shame, and sat down at the right hand of the throne of God. Consider him who endured such opposition from sinful men, so that you will not grow weary and lose heart. In your struggle against sin, you have not yet resisted to the point of shedding your blood. And you have forgotten that word of encouragement that addresses you as sons: "My son, do not make light of the Lord's discipline, and do not lose heart when he rebukes you, because the Lord disciplines those he loves, and he punishes everyone he accepts as a son." Endure hardship as discipline; God is treating you as sons. For what son is not disciplined by his father? If you are not disciplined (and everyone undergoes discipline), then you are illegitimate children and not true sons. Moreover, we have all had human fathers who disciplined us and

> we respected them for it. How much more should we submit to the Father of our spirits and live! Our fathers disciplined us for a little while as they thought best; but God disciplines us for our good, that we may share in his holiness. No discipline seems pleasant at the time, but painful. Later on, however, it produces a harvest of righteousness and peace for those who have been trained by it. Therefore, strengthen your feeble arms and weak knees. "Make level paths for your feet," so that the lame may not be disabled, but rather healed (Hebrews 12:1-13).

We tend to run from discipline, or we view it as punishment. But the punishment that brought us peace was undeservedly placed upon Christ as He hung on the cross. God has no desire to punish us, but He does discipline us out of love. Punishment is payback—You did this; therefore, here's what you get. But discipline is always administered with restoration in mind, and to bring out an individual's full potential—to train the loved one to maximize his purpose—to prepare him for the assignment to which he's been called. Though imperfect human beings often wrongly discipline in anger—which, left uncorrected, leads to abuse—we must realize that God is never this way with His children.

The model of our study, to which we'll make personal application throughout the rest of this chapter, is Jesus's final week on earth.

The Praise of Palm Sunday

One week before Christ's resurrection, He descended the Mount of Olives on a donkey. This occasion is referred to as Palm Sunday because the people placed their cloaks and palm branches in the path of the donkey, ahead of Christ as He rode along.

There were loud praises as the crowd shouted "Hosanna!" and waved palm branches in the air; for them, this was a moment of exhilaration! Their Messiah, the King of the Jews, was riding into Jerusalem to assume the throne (they thought) and, in a real sense, to overthrow the power and oppression of Rome. But Jesus knew better. He was about to begin the greatest trial of His life—the betrayal, the arrest, the rejection, and His own crucifixion and death.

The triumphal entry was marked by joyous expressions of praise and worship, followed by a season of intense physical and spiritual struggle—and death. It is only *after* the suffering and death that the resurrection comes.

Many believers want resurrection life. They are avid praisers and worshipers, but they view suffering and death as an interruption along the way. When trials come, they often become resentful or disillusioned, and they're even tempted to give up! Some feel like they've failed, so they retreat. Others become angry with God for allowing the suffering.

The truth is, though, believers are called to suffer—called to die, as demonstrated in the following scriptures…

"Your attitude should be the same as that of Christ Jesus: Who, being in very nature God, did not consider equality with God something to be grasped, but made himself nothing, taking the very nature of a servant, being made in human likeness. And being found in appearance as a man, he humbled himself and became obedient to death—even death on a cross!" (Philippians 2:5–8).

"For it has been granted to you on behalf of Christ not only to believe on him, but also to suffer for him" (Philippians 1:29).

The disciples were no different than us, as the events of the Passion unfolded. Many misunderstood, became disillusioned, and fell away as a result of the betrayal, arrest, rejection, crucifixion, and death of Christ. Even Peter denied Christ three times! And many of Jesus's former followers became the very ones who called for His crucifixion!

The heat of the moment caused true internal character to be displayed, just as heat causes impurities to rise to the surface during the purification of fine metals. The hotter the flames, the more the uncommitted dropped like flies. Crowds quickly turned to handfuls.

Consider Peter's words…

"Praise be to the God and Father of our Lord Jesus Christ! In his great mercy he has given us new birth into a living hope through the resurrection of Jesus Christ from the dead, and into an inheritance that can never perish, spoil or fade—kept in heaven for you, who through faith are shielded by God's power until the coming of the salvation that is ready to be revealed in the last time. In this you greatly rejoice, though now for a little while you may have had to suffer grief in all kinds of trials. *These have come so that your faith—of greater worth than gold, which perishes even though refined by fire—may by proved genuine* and may result in praise, glory and honor when Jesus Christ is revealed" (1 Peter 1:3–7, emphasis added).

Verse 7 affirms that our faith is of greater worth than gold. Suffering and grief and all kinds of trials will serve the divine purpose of refining our precious faith, and will cause that faith to be genuine.

For Jesus, the garden of suffering sat right between the praise and worship of the triumphal entry and the power of the resurrection. It was in the garden—the "womb of suffering" for Christ—that incredible wrestling took place—wrestling over the death of His will and the complete surrender of His life to God's supreme care and authority.

Too often, we believers want to bypass the gardens and tombs in our lives. We enjoy praise and worship—the triumph. We desire newness of life, freedom from bondage, and the feeling of being transformed more into the image of Jesus, but we buck against grief of the garden and death of the tomb. We want to bypass the very thing that's most instrumental in bringing to pass the resurrection we desire!

The Beauty of Worship and the Fire of Suffering

What does all of this have to do with praise and worship? Much in every way! Let's consider, for a moment, the fragrance and beauty of our worship. In the old covenant system, incense was often burned to become pleasingly fragrant. Such incense was taken by the priest into the holy of holies to be presented to the Lord. In scripture, incense is considered a "type" of the prayers and worship of New Testament believers.

Now incense has a pleasing fragrance before it is burned, but the richness and fullness of that fragrance is released only as the fire is added. In our lives as well, our prayers and worship are pleasing and acceptable through the sacrifice of Jesus Christ. But when the fires of life are applied, and we, His children, cry out in prayer and worship, *the full fragrance of our broken lives is released, and character is burned into the depth of our beings!*

Consider how quickly many desperation prayers get answered. Could it be that as we pray—as we praise and worship in the midst of the fire, we are releasing a fragrance unto God that is far more precious and beautiful than prayer and worship without the fire? Could it be that our crisis, trial, or unfavorable circumstance is actually allowing a fuller fragrance of brokenness to be released as we lift worship offerings to the Lord? I believe so.

The Commitment of Worship and Pain of Suffering

Commitment and *value*: these are two very important words. And *your commitment to something will never exceed the value you place upon it.* Read the account of Mary, as recorded in Mark chapter 14…

> Now the Passover and the Feast of Unleavened Bread were only two days away, and the chief priests and the teachers of the law were looking for some sly way to arrest Jesus and kill him. "But not during the Feast," they said, "or the people may riot." While he was in Bethany, reclining at the table in the home of a man known as Simon the Leper, a woman came with an alabaster jar of very expensive perfume, made of pure nard. She broke the jar and poured the perfume on his head. Some of those present were saying indignantly to one another, "Why this waste of perfume? It could have been sold for more than a year's wages and the money given to the poor." And they rebuked her harshly. "Leave her alone," said Jesus. "Why are you bothering her? She has done a beautiful thing to me.

> The poor you will always have with you, and you can help them any time you want. But you will not always have me. She did what she could. She poured perfume on my body beforehand to prepare for my burial. I tell you the truth, wherever the gospel is preached throughout the world, what she has done will also be told, in memory of her." Then Judas Iscariot, one of the Twelve, went to the chief priests to betray Jesus to them. They were delighted to hear this and promised to give him money. So he watched for an opportunity to hand him over (Mark 14:1–11).

Here, we have an incident taking place in the home of Simon the leper (previously healed by Jesus). We know, from John's account of the event, that the woman is Mary, the sister of Martha and Lazarus (previously raised from the dead by Jesus). While reclining in Jesus's presence, Mary takes hold of an alabaster jar filled with expensive nard (a type of ointment), worth approximately one year's wages. (In contemporary terms, this could be between $40,000 and $50,000!) She breaks the container and pours its expensive contents upon Jesus, as an act of love, sacrifice, and devotion. We discover later that this is prophetic, as she is actually anointing Jesus's body for burial. The other individuals in the room become indignant (i.e., filled with violent displeasure) because they view the whole exercise as an awful waste. Jesus, however, commends her. What a contrast!

As I think of earthen vessels, containers filled with priceless treasures, I can't help but recall the words of Paul in 2 Corinthians 4…

"But we have this treasure [the life and power of Christ] in jars of clay [our humanity] to show that this all-surpassing power is from God and not from us" (2 Corinthians 4:7).

We have a pure and priceless treasure within us—the Spirit of God, the substance of Christ—worth far more than a year's wages! Are we willing that these containers (the alabaster jars of our lives—our expectations, goals, dreams, and securities) be broken, so that the beautiful treasure of Christ in us can be poured out for God's glory?

Remember, *your commitment to something will never exceed the value you place upon it.* How much do you value Christ and His purposes being worked out in your life? Do you place a higher value upon God receiving glory from the brokenness of your life, or upon your own preservation as a container?

If you place more value on Christ and God's glory than your own preservation, you will have no problem spending yourself on Him and truly letting your container be broken. Think about this in the context of the petty, internal struggles we have with wholehearted praise and worship. We are far too worried about our reputations and how others will view us. Friend, Jesus is in the room! Get the jar of your life—your reputation—and break it! Anoint Jesus with its contents, that the life of Christ—the Spirit of God within you—can be released!

Jesus says in Luke 9:23: "If anyone would come after me, he must *deny himself* and take up his cross daily and follow me" (emphasis added).

Paul says in 1 Corinthians 15:31: "I *die* every day" (emphasis added).

In 1 Corinthians 15:36: "What you sow does not come to life unless it *dies*" (emphasis added).

And in Galatians 2:20: "I have been *crucified* with Christ and I no longer live, but Christ lives in me. The life I live in the body, I live by faith in the Son of God, who loved me and gave himself for me" (emphasis added).

You have awesome treasure within you. The greatest waste of that treasure is holding onto it—keeping it to yourself—shutting it up tightly within your vessel of clay. The Spirit within you wants to be released, liberated, and allowed to burst forth and radiate with the glory of God!

The Spirit within you *can't wait* for you to forgive your enemies, live in holiness and purity, and rest in the peace of Almighty God. But it's going to take a death—the breaking of the jar. It will take an act of your will to yield to the Spirit's promptings. Mary could have withheld her treasure for another day—waited for a different occasion. Jesus could have come and gone that evening, and the alabaster jar could have remained on the shelf, untouched. Friend, talk about waste! That would have been the greatest waste! But she didn't put it off. She didn't ignore her heart, in spite of what her mind might have concluded. She "offended" the container. Broke it. Withheld nothing. Poured all of its precious contents upon her Master and Savior.

We, too, have to be willing to die to ourselves. Our vessels are broken through suffering and trials—through the circumstances of life. We must be willing to allow our flesh to be offended and our dignity to be leveled. We must be willing to break ourselves open before the Lord in praise and worship, spilling the contents of our heart, and like Mary, letting Jesus deal with the critics!

Consider this: Judas assessed the value of his relationship with Jesus at thirty pieces of silver. But Mary assessed the value of her relationship with Jesus at a much higher cost; it was worthy of everything she had. What a contrast! Remember, *your commitment to something will never exceed the value you place upon it.*

Consider Paul's words to the Philippians, concerning his hardship and imprisonment...

"For I know that through your prayers and the help given by the Spirit of Jesus Christ, what has happened to me *will turn out for my deliverance.* I eagerly expect and hope that I will in no way be ashamed, but will have sufficient courage so that now as always Christ will be exalted in my body, *whether by life or by death.* For to me, to live is Christ and to die is gain" (Philippians 1:19–21, emphasis added).

Now notice what he says to the Philippian believers as they also face a garden experience...

"For it has been granted to you on behalf of Christ not only to believe on him, but also to suffer for him" (Philippians 1:29).

What was Paul's advice to this group of people as they traveled through the "womb of suffering"?

Well, like it or not, he affirmed that they were going to suffer. There's no doubt about that! In essence, he said, "Times will intensify. They'll get bad. But cling to Jesus, even if it means death. And don't be afraid to know Him in *that way*—to share in the fellowship of His sufferings. And, Philippians, no matter what happens, in the midst of intense struggle and trial, keep your conduct pure. Don't be selfish. Don't start complaining and arguing. But stand firm in one spirit, moving forward in the faith as one man."

The heat is on for us, too, in this final hour. Trials will intensify as long as we are on this earth. We may choose, while in the "womb of suffering," to become critical by being resistant to His loving discipline and challenging tests. We could, in turn, never realize on the outside what God has already made us to be on the inside. We could abort God's best for our lives and ministries. But if we choose to submit to the process and die to ourselves, we will see our lives burst forth into ever-increasing maturity, and our praise and worship will really increase in depth and substance. Paul goes on to say (in paraphrase), "Pursue your purpose in Christ! Run toward the goal! Don't give any ground back to the enemy! Don't be diverted by suffering or trials! Live up to what you've attained!" Then, he offers the following encouragement to these Philippian worshipers…

"He who began a good work in you will carry it on to completion until the day of Christ Jesus" (Philippians 1:6).

"Therefore, my dear friends, as you have always obeyed—not only in my presence, but now much more in my absence—continue to work out your salvation with fear and trembling, for it is God who works in you to will and to act according to his good purpose" (Philippians 2:12–13).

See similar promises in scriptures to the right (Psalm 57:2, Psalm 138:8, and Proverbs 19:21).

> Psalm 57:2: "I cry out to God Most High, to God, who fulfills his purpose for me."
>
> Psalm 138:8: "The LORD will fulfill his purpose for me; your love, O LORD, endures forever—do not abandon the works of your hands."
>
> Proverbs 19:21: "Many are the plans in a man's heart, but it is the Lord's purpose that prevails."

The Womb of Suffering

The pain is never pleasant, but don't hate the process. It is the very thing that will bring your life to a deeper level of maturity! If you find yourself in the "womb of suffering," it is there that your praise and worship will gain maturity and depth of character. *Anybody* can shout "Hosanna!" in the crowd during a triumphal procession, but what about after the people have all disappeared, and you've found yourself in the darkness at midday, and your dreams and hopes have been crucified? How about in the midst of unbearable trials and inevitable defeat, when the smell of death lingers? *Then*, who will cling to the cross? *Then*, who will lift his or her voice and worship God? I would venture to say that is a place of true worship.

There *is* resurrection and restoration coming to your church and the larger Body of Christ. We've learned how to cry "Hosanna!" We've celebrated and worshiped our way right down the mountain, through the streets of Jerusalem, and into the midst of the fire. Now, we find ourselves in the garden of agony, wrestling over the true submission of *our will* to *God's will*. We find ourselves at the feet of our accusers and hear demonic, oppressive voices threatening and intimidating us. We may find that our closest friends are rejecting us, as Peter did Jesus. "I thought they were on my side! Now they've turned away from me because of the stand I'm taking for Christ!" And we may even find that some who used to praise us are now shouting "Crucify!"

Sooner or later, you will find yourself facing a cross, and, simultaneously, your own selfishness. You will feel the weight of that cross tearing at your back. You will feel your knees start to quiver, and you will have to decide, "Am I going to die to self, or compromise and turn back?" Will you second-guess your commitment? Will you justify half-heartedness? In the midst of your trials, will you allow your "hosannas" to grow still? Will you turn on others and become argumentative, bitter, or fault-finding? Or will you lift up your head, through the sweat and blood dripping from your brow, and fix your eyes on Jesus, the Author and Finisher of your faith—and for the joy set before you, *endure the cross*?

I'm not talking about stirring up will power or becoming tougher, in order to preserve "self." I'm talking about letting "self" die and walking in the life Christ has prepared for you. I'm talking about letting the "self-life" go and walking in the "Christ-life" that longs to be manifest in you. Though your body may be wasting away, your spirit leaps for joy, knowing that *in* your suffering and hardships, you will reap a great reward!

Friend, be assured, there *will come* a resurrection. There *will come* new life. It will be birthed when you least expect it. Only don't give up! Learn to worship the Lord in the "womb of suffering!"

I close with this encouraging statement from the apostle Paul…

"Let us not become weary in doing good, for at the proper time we will reap a harvest if we do not give up" (Galatians 6:9).

Summation

1. Pain is never fun. But we should rejoice in difficult times because the Lord is refining us and bringing greater depth and substance to our lives.
2. Various trials test our devotion and bring maturity to our praise and worship.
3. Because of God's great love for us, He disciplines us. But this discipline is always restorative and life-producing.
4. Praise is easy when circumstances in our lives are wonderful. But what about during tough times? It is easy to praise at the resurrection, but worship in the garden is most difficult.
5. The fire of suffering releases the full fragrance of our praise and worship.
6. Our commitment to something will never exceed the value we place upon it.
7. As we allow the containers of our lives to be broken, the treasure of "Christ in us" flows out.

Devotional Exercise

Take a few moments to reflect on how you've grown as a worshiper.

Next time you face a trial of any kind, *choose* to focus on God in the midst of it. Don't allow the enemy to bring defeat, but, instead, offer up a sacrifice of praise and worship.

Study Guide Questions—Chapter 12

1. In your own words, what is the significance of this chapter's title, "Worshiping in the Womb of Suffering"?
2. Why should you consider trials pure joy, according to James 1:2–4?
3. Explain the difference between punishment and discipline.
4. Why do you suppose some in the crowd who shouted "hosanna" at the triumphal entry crucified Jesus less than a week later?
5. When you face trials, how do you normally respond? Do you withdraw? Do you get angry or frustrated? Do you begin to question yourself? How do you cope?
6. In your own words, explain how the fire of suffering brings a richer fragrance to your praise and worship.
7. What does this statement mean to you: "Your commitment to something will never exceed the value you place upon it"?
8. If you allow your vessel to be broken through trials and suffering, and, in that state of brokenness, willingly offer praise and worship to the Lord, in what ways might Christ shine forth from you? How might He receive glory?
9. What was most meaningful to you in this chapter?

Afterword

The church is at a crossroads, and we must make some decisions. Are we going to be people of His presence? Will we foster His kingdom purpose in these last days? Yes, the worship renewal has put praise and worship on the map for many churches, and there has been extensive teaching about God's kingdom in recent years. Still, I wonder if people are really worshiping in spirit and truth; and, at times, I wonder whose kingdom we're truly building.

The deterioration of spiritual fervor in God's house is evident. As I've traveled the United States, I've continually witnessed "performance" over "presence." Music is better than ever, sound systems are state-of-the-art, and stage lights rival some of the best concert venues. Yet something is missing. Where are the worshipers?

I've left many church services with holy discontentment. The stage was entirely set for a glorious encounter with God, but the experience fell short of a life-changing interaction with Him.

Yet there is hope. In fact, some extraordinary things are happening in the Body of Christ. And there's no better example I can point to than my home church, The House—in Modesto, California. Pastors Glen and Deborah Berteau have cultivated an atmosphere of revival and renewal here for over twenty years, and the result has been nothing less than phenomenal. I've seen thousands upon thousands of "unchurched" people become devoted followers of Jesus Christ. And in the process, these men and women have discovered how to be people of His presence, how to tap into God's kingdom purpose through authentic praise and worship!

Here are a few stories (names changed).

Rich stumbled into a church service several years ago, his life in shambles. He had grown up in church and was all-too-familiar with the sights and sounds of Sunday-morning worship, but years of drug and alcohol abuse had taken their toll. He wasn't even sure if he still believed in God. Yet, something was about to happen—for the better. As the congregation began singing songs of praise and worship, Rich felt a love he had never experienced, and the heart of this hardened sinner began to melt in God's presence. When an invitation was offered at the end of the service, Rich couldn't wait to respond. And like many others, Rich's life was forever changed at an altar that day.

Eager for a fresh start, Rich began attending a weekly men's meeting, where he learned what it means to be a man of God, but also, how to really worship the Father. Week after week, the men's pastor challenged every man in the room to go after God with all his heart—and each week, God showed up in power as men offered their very best worship.

I'll never forget one of the meetings. It had been a couple years since Rich's born-again experience, and I was the praise and worship leader that night. We were having an awesome time in God's presence, and at one point, I challenged everyone to take the next step. Little did I know that the place was about to erupt with exuberant praise. In a matter of seconds, Rich and several of the other men were at the altar, dancing with all of their might!

Later, after the meeting was over, Rich thanked me for challenging him to take that next step. He explained how his life had been full of so much pride and bitterness just a couple years prior, and he never would have *thought* about dancing like that back then. But now, he was experiencing joy and freedom, and nothing would hold back his praise!

Fast-forward to the present. Rich is currently a leader in the men's ministry, helping others find the same freedom he's found. When services are about to begin, Rich is one of the first men to the altar, eager to praise God with all of his might. There's currently a movement in our church, in fact, where men flood the altar area during times of praise and worship, and their sacrifice of praise seems to be the catalyst for breakthrough in the congregation and powerful encounters with God. I've never seen anything quite like it!

Turning to another story, Ashley did not grow up in a Christian environment and probably attended church three or four times her whole life. Seemingly, Christians were fanatics who hated everyone outside of their circle. She was particularly annoyed by the "Jesus Freaks" at school, who constantly invited her to a weekly Bible study.

Though her parents were more-or-less loving, it seemed that Ashley never measured up to their high expectations. She wasn't good enough at school, sports, or just about everything else, it seemed. Moving into high school, she began to hang out with the wrong crowd and entered into sexual relationships with several boys, in an attempt to find the acceptance and approval she had longed for. When those relationships failed one by one, Ashley turned to self-mutilation (cutting herself) as a way to cope. By her junior year, she hated herself in every way and basically felt numb toward the world. At one point, she almost took her life.

Shortly after that suicide attempt, one of the Jesus Freaks invited her to Stadium (the church's youth service). To everyone's amazement, Ashley accepted the invitation. She couldn't get past the fact that all of these Christians seemed really happy and fulfilled. Deep down inside she longed for what they had, so why not give it a shot? After all, things couldn't get any worse.

Ashley found herself driving into the church parking lot at 7:05 p.m. that next Wednesday. She sat in her car for a few minutes, arguing with herself about going into the service. *What will people think of me? Is it even worth it, when I'm already late? Could this really be the answer?* Despite the tug-of-war, something was compelling her to get out of the car and walk up to that building. She could hear music as she approached the sanctuary entrance, and once inside, a flood of emotions came over her as she saw hundreds of young people lifting their voices in praise and worship. She didn't understand it all, but she knew she was "home." The girl who had invited her to the service ran over, gave her a big hug, and the two of them walked down to the altar, where Ashley's life was forever changed.

That particular night, the praise and worship time extended for almost an hour. When the worship leaders tried to end the last song of the set, young people in the crowd kept singing. This probably went on for twenty minutes. In a funny sort of way, I think God knew Ashley and others needed extra time in His presence that night. Major heart surgery was taking place, and true transformation was happening.

Now Ashley is an intern for the youth ministry and is enrolled in the campus college, SEU. She's preparing to be a pastor and works every week with young girls facing the same challenges she once faced. Her physical scars are a reminder of all God has brought her through, and her heart has truly been restored in His presence.

The final story is one of my favorites. Mary came from a traditional church background, where prayer was a very private discipline, and worship was extremely reserved. She didn't have a problem with people praying out loud or expressing themselves during times of praise and worship, but this woman in her mid-sixties preferred a much quieter experience—the way it had been most of her life—that is, until she began having health issues.

Shortly after her sixty-fifth birthday, doctors informed Mary that cancer was spreading rapidly through her body. Suddenly, her world was turned upside-down, and quieter prayers turned to passionate pleas. A coworker had told Mary many times about the ministry of The House and a weekly prayer meeting, where people had often received prayers for healing. At first, Mary wasn't interested, but over time, she grew desperate for a touch from God, and she seemed to be drawn to this particular meeting. Finally, after several weeks, Mary attended Monday House of Prayer.

She entered the sanctuary that night, and the atmosphere was electric as people were praising and worshiping with all of their might. This church service was different than any she had ever attended; there seemed to be strong faith in the air, and, in Mary's words, a heaviness lifted off of her that she had been carrying for the past several months, even as she walked into the room. Still, she was rather weak physically, so she sat and soaked everything in.

As is often the case, praise and worship extended for over an hour that night. The church sang passionately, and at one point, nearly everyone was lying prostrate on the floor, as the Spirit of God moved upon people's hearts. Moments of deep and intimate worship gave way to a season of breakthrough, as pastoral leadership felt led to pray for those with physical ailments. Recognizing the healing presence of God, people virtually ran to the altar for ministry. Still very weak, Mary indicated a desire to receive prayer, but she would need her friend's assistance in getting to the altar.

They hadn't taken two or three steps before Mary began to feel a burning sensation all over her body. The congregation was singing a well-known worship song about healing, and as the lyrics were repeated over and over, Mary could sense something powerful happening; fatigue and pain were giving way. Just as she reached the altar area, the congregation lifted up a shout of praise, thanking God in advance for the healing that was about to sweep over the crowd. Mary joined others in praising God, and what can only be described as a tidal wave of healing swept from one end of the room to the other. Suddenly, this quiet, reserved, elderly lady began jumping up and down, shouting, "I'm healed! I'm healed!" Doctors would later verify that the cancer was gone, and Mary was entirely in remission! It's another example of a life forever changed in the presence of God.

Now, we often see Mary on the front row with a great big smile on her face as praise and worship is about to begin. There she is, nearly seventy years old, worshiping God fervently alongside men and women less than half her age. Is she too old? Has her ship already sailed? Not a chance! Like so many others, Mary has simply said yes to God. She has joined countless individuals who can't settle for church-as-usual. She has experienced the genuine touch of God, and there's no turning back. She's become an extravagant worshiper!

I could share many other stories, but hopefully, these few ignite something in your heart. Yes, the church is at a significant crossroads, but there is hope! Christians are grabbing a hold of the truth about praise and worship. The House and other congregations all across the land are becoming worshiping congregations, and the enemy is losing ground. My prayer, as I close, is that you will feel the urgency of the hour—that you will see what's at stake—that you will do everything possible to position yourself alongside others who have purposed to be *people of His presence.*

Come quickly, Lord! But until that day, may we be found worshiping You wholeheartedly!